OLD–FASHIONED

HOLIDAY
RECIPES

DEBBIE MUMM

Publications International, Ltd.

Favorite Brand Name Recipes at www.fbnr.com

ISBN-13: 978-1-4127-2343-5
ISBN-10: 1-4127-2343-4

Library of Congress Control Number: 2005910383

Manufactured in China.

8 7 6 5 4 3 2 1

Microwave Cooking: Microwave ovens vary in wattage. Use the cooking times as guidelines and check for doneness before adding more time.

Preparation/Cooking Times: Preparation times are based on the approximate amount of time required to assemble the recipe before cooking, baking, chilling or serving. These times include preparation steps such as measuring, chopping and mixing. The fact that some preparations and cooking can be done simultaneously is taken into account. Preparation of optional ingredients and serving suggestions is not included.

CONTENTS

Santa's Express

Cocktail Meatballs

1 pound *each* ground beef and bulk pork or Italian sausage

1 cup cracker crumbs

1 cup *each* finely chopped onion and green bell pepper

½ cup milk

1 egg, beaten

2 teaspoons salt

1 teaspoon dried Italian seasoning

¼ teaspoon black pepper

1 cup ketchup

¾ cup packed brown sugar

½ cup (1 stick) butter or margarine

½ cup cider vinegar

¼ cup *each* lemon juice and water

1 teaspoon prepared yellow mustard

¼ teaspoon garlic salt

1. Preheat oven to 350°F. Combine beef, sausage, crumbs, onion, bell pepper, milk, egg, salt, Italian seasoning and black pepper in large bowl; mix well. Shape into 1-inch balls. Place on nonstick baking sheets. Bake 25 minutes or until browned.

2. Meanwhile, combine remaining ingredients in slow cooker; mix well. Cover; cook on HIGH until hot. Transfer meatballs to slow cooker; carefully stir to coat with sauce. Reduce heat to LOW. Cover; cook 2 hours.   *Makes 12 servings*

Cocktail Meatballs

Brandy-Soaked Scallops

1 pound bacon, cut in half crosswise

2 pounds small raw sea scallops

½ cup brandy

⅓ cup olive oil

2 tablespoons chopped fresh parsley

1 clove garlic, minced

1 teaspoon black pepper

½ teaspoon salt

½ teaspoon onion powder

1. Wrap 1 bacon slice around each scallop; secure with wooden toothpick, if necessary. Place wrapped scallops in 13×9-inch baking dish.

2. Combine brandy, oil, parsley, garlic, pepper, salt and onion powder in small bowl; mix well. Pour mixture over scallops; cover and marinate in refrigerator at least 4 hours.

3. Remove scallops from marinade; discard marinade. Arrange scallops on rack of broiler pan. Broil 4 inches from heat 7 to 10 minutes or until bacon is brown. Turn over; broil 5 minutes more or until scallops are opaque. Remove toothpicks before serving. *Makes 8 servings*

Artichoke and Crabmeat Party Dip

1 container (16 ounces) sour cream (2 cups)

1 packet (1 ounce) HIDDEN VALLEY® The Original Ranch® Dips Mix

1 can (14 ounces) artichoke hearts, rinsed, drained and chopped

¾ cup cooked crabmeat, rinsed and drained

2 tablespoons chopped red or green bell pepper

French bread slices, crackers or fresh vegetables, for dipping

Combine sour cream and dips mix. Stir in artichoke hearts, crabmeat and bell pepper. Chill 30 minutes. Serve with French bread, crackers or fresh vegetables.

Makes 3½ cups

Avocado Salsa

1 medium avocado, peeled and diced

1 cup chopped seeded peeled cucumber

1 cup chopped onion

1 Anaheim chili*, seeded and chopped

½ cup chopped fresh tomato

2 tablespoons chopped fresh cilantro

½ teaspoon salt

¼ teaspoon hot pepper sauce

Chili peppers can sting and irritate the skin. Wear rubber gloves when handling peppers and do not touch eyes. Wash hands after handling peppers.

1. Combine avocado, cucumber, onion, chili, tomato, cilantro, salt and hot pepper sauce in medium bowl; mix well.

2. Refrigerate salsa, covered, at least 1 hour to allow flavors to blend. Serve as a dip with tortilla chips, toasted pita triangles or cut-up fresh vegetables.

Makes about 4 cups salsa

Cream Puff Appetizers

½ cup water

¼ cup CRISCO® Butter Flavor Shortening or ¼ CRISCO® Butter Flavor Stick

½ cup PILLSBURY BEST® All-Purpose Flour

⅛ teaspoon salt

2 eggs

Shrimp Filling

1 package (3 ounces) cream cheese, softened

⅓ cup dairy sour cream

4 teaspoons cocktail sauce

¼ teaspoon dried tarragon leaves

⅛ teaspoon pepper

Dash garlic powder

2 cans (6¼ ounces each) tiny shrimp, rinsed, drained and chopped

1 can (8 ounces) water chestnuts, drained and finely chopped

2 tablespoons finely chopped scallions

Salt to taste

Chicken Filling

2 cups finely chopped cooked chicken

⅔ cup mayonnaise or salad dressing

½ cup finely chopped celery

⅓ cup finely chopped almonds

1 hard-cooked egg, finely chopped

1½ teaspoons lemon juice

¾ teaspoon salt

¼ teaspoon pepper

Preheat oven to 400°F. In medium saucepan combine water and CRISCO Butter Flavor. Heat to rolling boil. Add flour and salt, stirring until mixture forms a ball. Continue to cook and stir for 1 minute. Remove from heat. Add eggs all at once, beating until smooth.

Drop by ½-teaspoonfuls at least 1½ inches apart onto ungreased baking sheet. Bake at 400°F for 20 to 30 minutes, or until golden brown. Cool away from draft. Meanwhile, prepare one of the fillings.

Shrimp Filling

In medium mixing bowl blend cream cheese and sour cream. Stir in cocktail sauce, tarragon, pepper and garlic powder. Add shrimp, water chestnuts and scallions. Mix thoroughly. Cover and refrigerate for at least 30 minutes. Season to taste with salt.

Chicken Filling

In medium mixing bowl combine all ingredients. Mix thoroughly. Cover and refrigerate for at least 30 minutes.

To fill, cut off tops of cooled cream puffs. Remove soft dough from inside. Fill with desired filling. Replace tops.   *Makes 2 dozen*

Celebration Cheese Ball

    2 packages (8 ounces each) cream cheese, softened
    ⅓ cup mayonnaise
    ¼ cup grated Parmesan cheese
    2 tablespoons finely chopped carrot
    1 tablespoon finely chopped red onion
1½ teaspoons prepared horseradish
    ¼ teaspoon salt
    ½ cup chopped pecans or walnuts
       Assorted crackers and breadsticks

1. Combine all ingredients except pecans and crackers in medium bowl. Cover and refrigerate until firm.

2. Shape cheese mixture into a ball; roll in pecans. Wrap cheese ball in plastic wrap and refrigerate at least 1 hour. Serve with assorted crackers and breadsticks.   *Makes about 2½ cups*

Holiday Meat and Vegetable Kabobs

1 cup fresh pearl onions

⅓ cup olive oil

2 tablespoons balsamic vinegar

1 tablespoon TABASCO® brand Pepper Sauce

1 tablespoon dried basil leaves

2 large cloves garlic, crushed

1 teaspoon salt

1 pound boneless skinless chicken breasts

1 pound boneless beef sirloin

2 large red peppers, cored, seeded and cut into ¾-inch pieces

1 large green pepper, cored, seeded and cut into ¾-inch pieces

1 large zucchini, cut into ¾-inch pieces

Soak 3 dozen 4-inch-long wooden skewers in water overnight. Bring pearl onions and enough water to cover to a boil in 1-quart saucepan over high heat. Reduce heat to low. Cover and simmer 3 minutes or until onions are tender. Drain. When cool enough to handle, peel away outer layer of skin from onions.

Combine oil, vinegar, TABASCO® Sauce, basil, garlic and salt in medium bowl. Pour half of mixture into another bowl. Cut chicken and beef into ¾-inch pieces and place in bowl with TABASCO® Sauce mixture, tossing well to coat. In remaining bowl of TABASCO® Sauce mixture, toss pearl onions, red and green peppers and zucchini. Let stand at least 30 minutes, tossing occasionally.

Preheat broiler. Skewer 1 piece of chicken or beef and 1 piece each of red pepper, green pepper, onion and zucchini onto each wooden skewer. Broil 4 to 6 minutes, turning occasionally.

Makes 3 dozen kabobs

Honey Holiday Wraps

Prep Time: 30 minutes
Cook Time: 15 minutes

- 1 box frozen puff pastry sheets, thawed according to package directions
- 1 egg, beaten
- ¼ cup Honey Mustard Sauce (see recipe below)
- ½ pound JENNIE-O TURKEY STORE® Deli Homestyle Honey Cured Turkey Breast, thinly sliced and finely diced
- ¼ cup walnuts, toasted and chopped
- 4 ounces Brie cheese, cut into 18 pieces

Preheat oven to 375°F. Remove pastry sheets from box and cut each into 9 smaller squares. Brush squares with egg wash and drizzle each with a little honey mustard sauce. Toss diced JENNIE-O TURKEY STORE® Homestyle Honey Cured Turkey Breast with walnuts; place about 1 teaspoon turkey mixture in center of each pastry square. Top with piece of Brie cheese. Fold pastry over diagonally to form triangle, pressing edges to seal. Then pinch together two corners on folded edge of pastry to form tortellini shape. Place wraps on baking sheet. Bake at 375°F degrees for 15 to 18 minutes. Allow to cool slightly before serving. Serve with more honey mustard sauce, if desired.

Makes 18 wraps

Honey Mustard Sauce: Mix together 2 tablespoons Dijon mustard and 2 tablespoons honey. *Makes ¼ cup*

Serving Suggestions: Any variety of JENNIE-O TURKEY STORE® turkey or chicken breast can be used in this recipe. Try apple butter or pesto sauce instead of honey mustard.

Honey-Nut Glazed Brie

8 ounces Brie cheese (wedge or round)

¼ cup I CAN'T BELIEVE IT'S NOT BUTTER!® Spread

1 cup coarsely chopped walnuts

¼ teaspoon ground cinnamon (optional)

⅛ teaspoon ground nutmeg (optional)

2 tablespoons honey

2 large green and/or red apples, cored and thinly sliced

Arrange cheese on serving platter; set aside.

In 10-inch nonstick skillet, melt I Can't Believe It's Not Butter!® Spread over medium-high heat and stir in walnuts until coated. Stir in cinnamon and nutmeg until blended. Stir in honey and cook, stirring constantly, 2 minutes or until mixture is bubbling. Immediately pour over cheese. Serve hot with apples.   *Makes 8 servings*

Variations: Arrange cheese on microwave-safe plate and top with cooked nut mixture. Microwave at HIGH (100% power) 1 minute or until cheese is warm. Or, arrange cheese in 1-quart shallow casserole and top with cooked nut mixture. Bake at 350°F for 10 minutes or until Brie just begins to melt. Serve hot with apples.

When properly ripened, Brie's creamy soft interior will "ooze" out when its edible white mold rind is cut after it's baked.

Hot Cheesy Spinach & Artichoke Dip

Prep Time: 10 minutes
Cook Time: 35 minutes

- 1 package (10 ounces) frozen chopped spinach, thawed and squeezed dry
- 1 package (8 ounces) cream cheese, softened
- ¾ cup HELLMANN'S® or BEST FOODS® Real Mayonnaise
- 1½ cups shredded cheddar or Monterey Jack cheese (about 6 ounces), divided
- 1 package KNORR® Recipe Classics™ Vegetable Soup, Dip and Recipe Mix
- 1 can (14 ounces) artichoke hearts, drained and chopped
- 1 can (8 ounces) water chestnuts, drained and chopped
- 2 cloves garlic, finely chopped

Preheat oven to 350°F.

In medium bowl, combine all ingredients except ½ cup cheddar cheese. Spoon into 2-quart casserole, then top with remaining ½ cup cheddar cheese.

Bake 35 minutes or until heated through. Serve, if desired, with toasted French baguette rounds, sliced garlic bread, corn or tortilla chips or vegetable dippers.   *Makes about 4 cups dip*

Spanakopita Dip: Substitute feta cheese for the cheddar and eliminate the artichoke hearts. Spoon into mini phyllo cups and bake 8 minutes or until filling puffs.

Quick Pickled Green Beans

½ pound (3½ cups loosely packed) whole green beans

½ red bell pepper, cut into strips (optional)

1 jalapeño* or other hot pepper, cut into strips

1 large clove garlic, cut in half

1 bay leaf

1 cup white wine vinegar

1 cup water

½ cup white wine

1 tablespoon sugar

1 tablespoon salt

1 tablespoon whole coriander seeds

1 tablespoon mustard seeds

1 tablespoon whole peppercorns

Jalapeño peppers can sting and irritate the skin. Wear rubber gloves when handling peppers and do not touch eyes. Wash hands after handling.

1. Wash green beans; remove stem ends. Place in glass dish just large enough to hold green beans and 2½ cups liquid. Add bell pepper strips, if desired. Tuck jalapeño, garlic and bay leaf between beans.

2. Place remaining ingredients in medium saucepan. Heat to a boil; stir to dissolve sugar and salt. Reduce heat; simmer 5 minutes. Pour mixture over green beans, making sure beans are fully submerged in liquid. If not, add additional hot water to cover.

3. Cover; refrigerate at least 24 hours. Remove and discard bay leaf before serving. Flavor improves in 48 hours and beans may be kept refrigerated for up to five days. Remove beans from liquid before serving. *Makes 6 servings*

Seasoned Snack Mix

⅔ CRISCO® Butter Flavor Stick or ⅔ cup CRISCO® Butter Flavor Shortening

¾ cup grated Parmesan cheese

2 teaspoons Italian seasoning

2 teaspoons Worcestershire sauce

¾ teaspoon garlic salt

¼ teaspoon onion powder

¼ teaspoon cayenne pepper

3 cups bite-size rice squares cereal

2 cups round toasted oat cereal

2 cups oyster crackers

2 cups pretzel sticks

1 can (7 ounces) Spanish peanuts

Salt, to taste

Preheat oven to 325°F. In Dutch oven melt CRISCO Butter Flavor. Remove from heat.

Stir in Parmesan cheese, Italian seasoning, Worcestershire sauce, garlic salt, onion powder and cayenne pepper.

Add rice squares, toasted oat cereal, oyster crackers, pretzel sticks and peanuts. Season with salt. Toss to coat. Spread on 17½×12×1-inch jelly-roll pan.

Bake at 325°F for 15 to 18 minutes or until toasted and golden brown, stirring once after 10 minutes. Cool. Store in covered container.

Makes 10 cups

Spinach-Cheese Appetizers

¼ cup olive oil

½ cup chopped onion

2 eggs

2 packages (8 ounces each) feta cheese, drained and crumbled

3 packages (10 ounces each) frozen chopped spinach, thawed and squeezed dry

½ cup minced fresh parsley

2 tablespoons chopped fresh oregano *or* 1 teaspoon dried oregano

Freshly grated nutmeg

Salt and black pepper

1 package (16 ounces) frozen phyllo dough, at room temperature

1 cup (2 sticks) butter or margarine, melted

1. Preheat oven to 375°F. Heat oil in small skillet over medium-high heat. Add onion; cook and stir until translucent. Beat eggs in large bowl; stir in onion, feta cheese, spinach, parsley and oregano. Season with nutmeg, salt and pepper.

2. Remove phyllo from package; unroll and place on large sheet of waxed paper. Fold phyllo crosswise into thirds. Use scissors to cut along folds into thirds. Cover phyllo with large sheet of plastic wrap and damp clean kitchen towel. Lay 1 strip of phyllo at a time on a flat surface and brush with melted butter. Fold strip in half lengthwise; brush with butter again. Place rounded teaspoonful of spinach filling on 1 end of strip; fold over one corner to make triangle. Continue folding end to end, as you would fold a flag, keeping edges straight. Brush top with butter. Repeat process until all filling is used.

3. Place triangles in single layer, seam side down, on baking sheet. Bake 20 minutes or until lightly browned. Serve warm.

Makes 5 dozen appetizers

Sizzlin' Shrimp

Prep Time: 5 minutes
Cook Time: 5 minutes

⅓ cup *Frank's® RedHot®* Original Cayenne Pepper Sauce
2 tablespoons olive oil
2 tablespoons butter
¾ teaspoon garlic powder
¾ teaspoon chili powder
1 pound raw large shrimp, shelled and deveined

1. Combine *Frank's RedHot* Sauce, oil, butter, garlic powder and chili powder in medium skillet. Heat over high heat until sauce is bubbly, stirring often.

2. Add shrimp; cook and stir 3 to 5 minutes or until shrimp are opaque and coated with sauce. *Makes 6 servings*

New Year's Toast Dip

2 packages (3 ounces each) cream cheese, softened
½ cup half-and-half or milk
⅓ cup mayonnaise
⅔ cup chopped crabmeat
2 tablespoons chopped green onion
2 teaspoons dry ranch salad dressing mix
Sliced green olives
Assorted fresh vegetables

1. Beat cream cheese in small bowl with electric mixer at medium speed until fluffy; beat in half-and-half and mayonnaise. Stir in crabmeat, onion and salad dressing mix. Refrigerate 1 hour or until serving time.

2. Spoon dip into martini glass or other glass or goblet with wide opening; garnish with olive slices. Serve with assorted fresh vegetables. *Makes about 2 cups dip*

Sausage Roll-Ups

Filling

¼ pound ground seasoned sausage, crumbled

½ cup chopped mushrooms

3 tablespoons chopped onion

2 tablespoons finely chopped celery

1 tablespoon chopped stuffed green olives

2 teaspoons PILLSBURY BEST® All-Purpose Flour

Dough

1 cup PILLSBURY BEST® All-Purpose Flour

1 teaspoon baking powder

1 teaspoon dried parsley flakes

¼ teaspoon salt

¼ cup CRISCO® Butter Flavor Shortening or ¼ CRISCO® Butter Flavor Stick, well chilled

¼ cup milk

Topping

2 tablespoons CRISCO® Butter Flavor Shortening, melted

Paprika

For filling, in small skillet combine sausage, mushrooms, onion, celery and olives. Cook and stir over medium-high heat until sausage is no longer pink. Stir in flour. Remove from heat. Set aside.

Preheat oven to 350°F. Lightly grease baking sheet. Set aside.

For dough,* in medium mixing bowl combine flour, baking powder, parsley flakes and salt. Cut in well-chilled CRISCO Butter Flavor to form coarse crumbs. Add milk, mixing with fork until particles are moistened and cling together. Form dough into ball. On floured board, knead 8 to 10 times.

To assemble roll-ups

Roll dough into a 16×12-inch rectangle. Spread filling on dough. Starting with longer side, roll up tightly.**

Cut into ½-inch slices. Place on baking sheet. Brush with melted CRISCO Butter Flavor. Sprinkle lightly with paprika. Bake at 350°F for 15 to 18 minutes, or until firm. *Make 2½ dozen roll-ups*

*Dough may also be made in a food processor fitted with a metal blade. Pulse to mix.

**Recipe can be made a day ahead to this point. Wrap roll tightly in plastic wrap and refrigerate. When ready to bake, remove plastic wrap and proceed as directed.

Red Pepper & Cheddar Crostini

1 (1-pound) narrow loaf French bread

3 tablespoons olive oil

1 teaspoon minced garlic

1 cup roasted red peppers (blotted dry if canned)

¼ cup (lightly packed) grated CABOT® Extra Sharp Cheddar

1 tablespoon capers, well drained

Salt and ground black pepper to taste

2 hard-boiled eggs, finely chopped

2 tablespoons finely chopped fresh parsley

1. Preheat broiler. Cut bread into thin slices and arrange in single layer on baking sheets.

2. In small bowl, combine olive oil and garlic; brush mixture on tops of bread slices. Broil one sheet at a time until golden.

3. In food processor or blender, combine red peppers, cheese and capers; pulse until chopped but not puréed. Season with salt and pepper. In small bowl, combine chopped eggs and parsley.

4. Place heaping teaspoonful of red pepper and cheese topping on each crostini and sprinkle with some of chopped egg mixture.

Makes about 32 crostini

Recipe courtesy of Chef Doug Mack

Cranberry-Barbecue Chicken Wings

   3 pounds chicken wings
     Salt and black pepper
   1 container (12 ounces) cranberry-orange relish
   ½ cup barbecue sauce
   2 tablespoons quick-cooking tapioca
   1 tablespoon prepared mustard

1. Preheat broiler. Cut off and discard chicken wing tips. Cut each wing in half at joint. Place chicken on rack in broiler pan; season with salt and pepper. Broil 4 to 5 inches from heat for 10 to 12 minutes or until browned, turning once. Transfer chicken to slow cooker.

2. Combine relish, barbecue sauce, tapioca and mustard in small bowl. Pour over chicken. Cover; cook on LOW 4 to 5 hours.

Makes about 16 servings

Crostini

   ¼ loaf whole wheat baguette (4 ounces)
   4 plum tomatoes
   1 cup (4 ounces) shredded part-skim mozzarella cheese
   3 tablespoons prepared pesto sauce
     Fresh basil leaves (optional)

1. Preheat oven to 400°F. Slice baguette into 16 very thin, diagonal slices. Slice each tomato lengthwise into 4 (¼-inch-thick) slices.

2. Place baguette slices on nonstick baking sheet. Top each slice with 1 tablespoon cheese, then 1 slice tomato. Bake about 8 minutes or until bread is lightly toasted and cheese is melted.

3. Remove from oven. Top each crostini with about ½ teaspoon pesto sauce. Garnish with fresh basil. Serve warm.

Makes 16 appetizers

Creamy Hot Reuben Dip

4 tablespoons CRISCO® Butter Flavor Stick or 4 tablespoons
CRISCO® Butter Flavor shortening

1 large onion, finely diced

½ pound corned beef, sliced and shredded

1 (8-ounce) package cream cheese, cubed

2 cups grated Swiss cheese

1½ cups sauerkraut, drained and chopped

½ cup mayonnaise

½ cup ketchup

2 tablespoons sweet pickle relish

2 tablespoons dill pickle relish

Melt CRISCO Butter Flavor in heavy 4-quart saucepan. Add onion
and cook until golden brown. Add corned beef; cook over medium
heat 3 minutes, stirring often. Drain fat.

Add cream cheese, 1 cube at a time, stirring after each addition. Add
cheese, sauerkraut, mayonnaise, ketchup and pickle relish.

Stir until cheeses are melted and ingredients are well blended. Serve in
fondue pot or chafing dish with toasted mini rye triangles.

Makes 6 to 8 servings

For toasted mini triangles, cut cocktail
rye bread slices diagonally in half.
Broil 6 to 8 inches from heat 30 to
45 seconds or until lightly toasted.

Eggplant Caviar

2 cups eggplant, fire roasted, finely chopped*

1 cup zucchini, fire roasted, finely chopped*

½ cup red bell pepper, fire roasted, finely chopped*

½ cup yellow bell pepper, fire roasted, finely chopped*

½ cup onions, fire roasted, finely chopped*

1 tablespoon plus 1 teaspoon garlic, fire roasted, finely chopped*

¼ cup plus 1 tablespoon cane syrup

¼ cup balsamic vinegar

1½ tablespoons Chef Paul Prudhomme's Vegetable Magic®

1 tablespoon Chef Paul Prudhomme's Magic Barbecue Seasoning®

1 tablespoon lemon juice

Make sure all vegetables are fully roasted to give a rich, smoky taste. Vegetables should be charred heavily in a very hot cast iron skillet or on a grill and then peeled.

Combine all ingredients and stir gently to combine.

Makes 4½ cups

Note: Eggplant caviar tastes great spread on melba toast, crackers, bagels and breads. It's also great as a relish with meat, vegetable and seafood dishes.

Fire-roasting the vegetables (grilling them over direct heat until their skins begin to blacken and blister) brings out their sweet, caramelized flavors.

Holiday Wassail

1 gallon MOTT'S® Apple Juice

1 quart orange juice

1 can (16 ounces) frozen pineapple juice, thawed

2 cups lemon juice

1 cup sugar

2 cinnamon sticks

2 teaspoons cloves

Place all ingredients in non-aluminum pan. Stir; heat to boiling. Simmer for 1 hour. Serve hot. *Makes 24 servings*

Ranch Buffalo Wings

½ cup butter or margarine, melted

¼ cup hot pepper sauce

3 tablespoons vinegar

24 chicken wing drummettes

1 packet (1 ounce) HIDDEN VALLEY® The Original Ranch® Salad Dressing & Seasoning Mix

½ teaspoon paprika

1 cup HIDDEN VALLEY® The Original Ranch® Dressing

Celery sticks

Preheat oven to 350°F. In small bowl, whisk together butter, pepper sauce and vinegar. Dip drummettes into butter mixture; arrange in single layer in large baking pan. Sprinkle with 1 package salad dressing & seasoning mix. Bake 30 to 40 minutes or until chicken is browned and juices run clear. Sprinkle with paprika. Serve with prepared salad dressing and celery sticks. *Makes 6 to 8 servings*

Sesame Pork Appetizers

1½ pounds pork tenderloin

½ cup plus 1 tablespoon dry sherry, divided

⅓ cup plus 1 tablespoon soy sauce, divided

½ cup honey

½ cup sesame seeds

1 tablespoon sesame oil

1 clove garlic, crushed

½ teaspoon grated fresh ginger

1 green onion, finely chopped

Spinach leaves

Place pork in large plastic bag. Combine ½ cup sherry and 1 tablespoon soy sauce; pour over pork, turning to coat. Seal bag. Marinate in refrigerator 1 to 2 hours, turning several times. Remove pork from marinade. Spread honey on plate. Spread sesame seeds in shallow dish. Roll pork in honey, then in sesame seeds. Arrange pork on roasting rack set in roasting pan. Bake at 350°F 25 to 30 minutes or until meat thermometer registers 155°F. Let stand 5 minutes. Slice thinly on the diagonal. Set aside.

Combine remaining ⅓ cup soy sauce, remaining 1 tablespoon sherry, sesame oil, garlic, ginger and onion in small bowl. Place bowl in center of serving platter. Surround the bowl with spinach leaves. Arrange pork slices on top.   *Makes 10 to 12 appetizer servings*

Favorite recipe from **National Pork Board**

Creamy Hot Chocolate

Prep Time: 8 to 10 minutes

  1 **(14-ounce) can EAGLE BRAND® Sweetened Condensed Milk
     (NOT evaporated milk)**
  ½ **cup unsweetened cocoa**
 1½ **teaspoons vanilla extract**
  ⅛ **teaspoon salt**
 6½ **cups hot water**
     Marshmallows (optional)

1. In large saucepan over medium heat, combine EAGLE BRAND®, cocoa, vanilla and salt; mix well.

2. Slowly stir in water. Heat through, stirring occasionally. Do not boil. Top with marshmallows (optional). Store covered in refrigerator.

Makes about 2 quarts

Microwave Directions: In 2-quart glass measure, combine all ingredients except marshmallows. Microwave at HIGH (100% power) 8 to 10 minutes, stirring every 3 minutes. Top with marshmallows, if desired. Store covered in refrigerator.

Tip: Hot chocolate can be stored in the refrigerator for up to 5 days. Mix well and reheat before serving.

Iced Swiss Chocolate Peppermint

  2 **cups strongly brewed Swiss Dutch Almond coffee**
  2 **tablespoons low-fat milk**
  2 **teaspoons sugar**
  ½ **teaspoon cocoa powder**
  1 **drop peppermint extract**

Combine all ingredients in blender or food processor; process until smooth. Pour over ice and serve immediately. Or refrigerate; stir well before serving over ice.

Makes 2 servings

*Favorite recipe from **The Sugar Association, Inc.***

Hot Mulled Cider

½ **gallon apple cider**

½ **cup packed light brown sugar**

1½ **teaspoons balsamic or cider vinegar**

1 **teaspoon vanilla**

1 **cinnamon stick**

6 **whole cloves**

½ **cup applejack (apple brandy) or bourbon (optional)**

Combine all ingredients except applejack in large saucepan; bring to a boil. Reduce heat to low; simmer, uncovered, 10 minutes. Remove from heat; stir in applejack, if desired. Pour into punch bowl.

Makes 16 servings

Hollyberry Fruit Dip

Prep Time: 10 minutes, plus chilling

1 **tub (8 ounces) softened cream cheese**

½ **cup KARO® Light Corn Syrup**

2 **tablespoons sugar**

½ **cup light sour cream**

1 **cup fresh or thawed frozen cranberries, chopped**

1 **tablespoon grated orange peel**

1. In small bowl with wire whisk or mixer at medium speed, beat cream cheese, corn syrup and sugar until fluffy. Blend in sour cream. Fold in cranberries and orange peel.

2. Chill.

3. Serve with fresh fruit dippers or shortbread cookies.

Makes about 2¼ cups

Easy Candied Nuts

Prep Time: 10 minutes
Cook Time: 30 minutes

  1 cup KARO® Light or Dark Corn Syrup
  ¼ cup (½ stick) butter or margarine
  2 egg whites
  ⅛ teaspoon salt
  ¼ cup sugar
  1 pound shelled mixed nuts (about 1¾ cups)

1. Begin heating oven to 325°F. Place butter in 15½×10½×1-inch jelly-roll pan and place in oven until melted. Remove pan from oven and set aside.

2. In medium bowl, with mixer, beat egg whites and salt until foamy. Add ¼ cup sugar and beat until soft peaks form. Beat in Karo. Stir in nuts, coating well. Pour into prepared pan; spread into single layer.

3. Bake 10 minutes. Stir nuts thoroughly. Return nuts to oven to bake 10 minutes longer; stir and bake 10 minutes more. Remove from oven. Stir for 5 minutes to break up nuts and cool slightly.

4. Continue stirring and breaking up nuts until lukewarm, 15 to 20 minutes. When cool enough to handle, separate into small pieces; cool completely. Store in airtight tins.   *Makes 5½ cups*

Merry Main Dishes

Roast Turkey with Pan Gravy

Sausage-Corn Bread Stuffing (page 31)

1 **fresh or thawed frozen turkey (12 to 14 pounds), giblets and neck reserved (discard liver or reserve for another use)**

2 **cloves garlic, minced**

½ **cup (1 stick) butter, melted**

Turkey Broth with Giblets (page 30)

1 **cup dry white wine or vermouth**

3 **tablespoons all-purpose flour**

Salt and black pepper

1. Preheat oven to 450°F. Prepare stuffing; stuff body and neck cavities of turkey loosely, if desired. Fold skin over openings; close with skewers. Tie legs together with cotton string or tuck through skin flap, if provided. Tuck wings under turkey. Place turkey on meat rack in shallow roasting pan. Stir garlic into butter. Insert ovenproof meat thermometer into thickest part of thigh not touching bone. Brush ⅓ of butter mixture evenly over turkey. Place turkey in oven. *Reduce oven temperature to 325°F.* Roast 4 to 5 hours (18 to 20 minutes per pound for unstuffed turkey, 22 to 24 minutes per pound for stuffed) or until internal temperature of turkey reaches 180°F. Brush with butter mixture after 1 hour and then after 1½ hours. Baste with pan juices every hour of roasting. If turkey is over-browning, tent with foil. Meanwhile, prepare Turkey Broth with Giblets.

continued on page 30

Roast Turkey with Pan Gravy

Roast Turkey with Pan Gravy, continued

2. Transfer turkey to cutting board; tent with foil. Let stand 15 minutes while preparing gravy.

3. Pour off and reserve juices from roasting pan. To deglaze pan, pour wine into pan. Place over burners; cook over medium-high heat, scraping up browned bits and stirring constantly 2 to 3 minutes or until mixture is reduced by about half.

4. Remove ⅓ cup fat from pan drippings to large saucepan; discard remaining fat. Add flour to saucepan. Cook, stirring constantly, over medium heat 1 minute. Slowly stir in 3 cups Turkey Broth, reserved pan juices and deglazed wine mixture from roasting pan. Cook over medium heat 10 minutes, stirring occasionally. Stir in reserved chopped giblets; heat through. Season to taste with salt and pepper.

Makes 12 servings and 3½ cups gravy

Creamy Turkey Gravy: Stir in 1 cup heavy cream with giblets; proceed as recipe directs. *Makes 4½ cups gravy*

Turkey Broth with Giblets

Reserved giblets and neck from turkey (discard liver or reserve for another use)

4 cups water

1 can (about 14 ounces) chicken broth

1 medium onion, cut into quarters

2 medium carrots, coarsely chopped

4 large sprigs fresh parsley

1 bay leaf

1 teaspoon dried thyme

10 whole black peppercorns

1. Combine giblets, neck, water and chicken broth in 3-quart saucepan; bring to a boil over high heat. Skim off foam. Stir in remaining ingredients. Reduce heat to low; simmer, uncovered, 1½ to 2 hours, stirring occasionally. (If liquid evaporates too quickly, add ½ cup water.) Cool to room temperature. Remove and discard bay leaf.

2. Strain broth. If broth measures less than 3 cups, add water to equal 3 cups. If broth measures more than 3 cups, bring to a boil; heat until reduced to 3 cups. Remove meat from neck and chop giblets finely. Cover broth and giblets separately; refrigerate.

Makes 3 cups broth

Sausage-Corn Bread Stuffing

½ **pound bulk pork sausage (regular or spicy)**

½ **cup (1 stick) butter or margarine**

2 **medium onions, chopped**

2 **cloves garlic, minced**

2 **teaspoons dried sage**

1 **teaspoon poultry seasoning**

1 **package (16 ounces) prepared dry corn bread crumbs**

¾ **to 1¼ cups chicken broth**

1. Brown sausage in large skillet over medium-high heat, stirring to separate meat. Drain on paper towels. Wipe skillet with paper towels. Melt butter in same skillet over medium heat until foamy. Add onions and garlic; cook and stir 10 minutes or until onions are softened. Stir in dried sage and poultry seasoning; cook 1 minute more.

2. Combine corn bread crumbs, sausage and onion mixture in large bowl. If stuffing is to be cooked in turkey, drizzle ¾ cup broth over stuffing; toss lightly until evenly moistened. (Stuffing may be prepared up to 1 day before using. *Do not stuff turkey until ready to roast.*) Stuff body and neck cavities loosely with stuffing. See page 28 for roasting instructions. If stuffing is to be cooked separately, drizzle 1¼ cups broth over stuffing; toss lightly until evenly moistened. Transfer to 3-quart casserole.

3. Preheat oven to 350°F. Bake 45 minutes (55 to 60 minutes if refrigerated) or until heated through. For drier stuffing, uncover during last 15 minutes of baking.

Makes 12 cups stuffing

Baked Pork Chops with Yams and Apples

Prep Time: 25 minutes
Total Time: 1¼ hours

- ½ **cup maple syrup**
- 1 **teaspoon minced garlic** *or* 1 **small clove garlic, peeled and minced**
- ½ **teaspoon ground ginger**
- ½ **teaspoon salt**
- ½ **teaspoon freshly ground black pepper**
- ¼ **teaspoon ground cinnamon**
- 1 **cup chicken stock or broth**
- 3 **tablespoons CRISCO® Oil***
- 4 **boneless loin pork chops, 1½ inches thick**
- 3 **medium yams or sweet potatoes, peeled and cut into 1-inch cubes**
- 2 **Granny Smith apples, quartered, cored and cut into 1-inch slices**
- **Parsley for garnish (optional)**

Use your favorite Crisco Oil.

1. Heat oven to 375°F. Combine maple syrup, garlic, ginger, salt, pepper, cinnamon and stock in small bowl. Mix well. Line roasting pan with heavy-duty aluminum foil.

2. Heat oil in large skillet on medium-high heat. Brown pork chops on both sides. Remove from pan.

3. Place chops in roasting pan. Add yams and apples. Pour maple syrup mixture over all. Bake uncovered at 375°F for 15 minutes. Remove pan from oven. Turn chops, yams and apples gently with spatula. Return to oven. Bake 10 minutes or until apples and yams are soft and pork is no longer pink in center. Serve immediately.   *Makes 4 servings*

Note: This dish can be prepared and baked up to one day in advance and refrigerated, tightly covered. Reheat the dish, covered, at 350°F for 15 minutes or until hot.

Orange-Cranberry Turkey Slices

- 1 **pound turkey breast slices or cutlets**
- **Salt and pepper**
- 2 **tablespoons margarine**
- 1 **cup fresh cranberries***
- ⅓ **cup orange juice**
- 2 **tablespoons packed brown sugar**
- ¼ **cup raisins**
- 2 **tablespoons chopped green onion**
- 2 **tablespoons orange-flavored liqueur or frozen orange juice concentrate**

If fresh cranberries are not available, omit brown sugar, reduce orange juice to 2 tablespoons and substitute ¼ cup canned whole cranberry sauce for 1 cup fresh cranberries.

1. Season turkey slices with salt and pepper. Brown turkey slices in margarine in skillet 2 to 3 minutes per side. Remove to platter; keep warm.

2. Add cranberries, orange juice and brown sugar to skillet; cook 5 minutes or until cranberries pop.

3. Stir in raisins, green onion and liqueur, if desired; heat through.

4. Serve sauce over warm turkey slices.   *Makes 6 servings*

*Favorite recipe from **National Turkey Federation***

Merry Main Dishes ~ 33

Beef Tenderloin with Roasted Vegetables

1 beef tenderloin roast (about 3 pounds), trimmed of fat

½ cup chardonnay or other dry white wine

½ cup reduced-sodium soy sauce

2 cloves garlic, sliced

1 tablespoon chopped fresh rosemary

1 tablespoon Dijon mustard

1 teaspoon dry mustard

1 pound small red or white potatoes, cut into 1-inch pieces

1 pound brussels sprouts

1 package (12 ounces) baby carrots

Pan Gravy (recipe follows)

Fresh rosemary (optional)

1. Place roast in large resealable food storage bag. Combine wine, soy sauce, garlic, rosemary, Dijon mustard and dry mustard in small bowl. Pour over roast. Seal bag; turn to coat. Marinate in refrigerator 4 to 12 hours, turning several times.

2. Preheat oven to 425°F. Spray 13×9-inch baking pan with nonstick cooking spray. Place potatoes, brussels sprouts and carrots in pan. Remove roast from marinade. Pour marinade over vegetables; toss to coat well. Cover vegetables with foil; roast 30 minutes. Stir.

3. Place tenderloin on vegetables. Roast, uncovered, 35 to 45 minutes or until internal temperature of roast reaches 135°F for medium-rare to 150°F for medium when tested with meat thermometer inserted into thickest part of tenderloin.

4. Transfer tenderloin to cutting board; tent with foil. Let stand 10 to 15 minutes before carving. (Internal temperature will continue to rise 5°F to 10°F during stand time.) Reserve drippings from roasting pan to make Pan Gravy.

5. Stir vegetables; continue baking if not tender. Slice tenderloin; arrange on serving platter with roasted vegetables and Pan Gravy. Garnish with fresh rosemary.   *Makes 10 servings*

Pan Gravy

Reserved drippings from roasting pan

3 tablespoons all-purpose flour

2 cups beef broth

¼ cup heavy whipping cream

½ teaspoon salt

¼ teaspoon black pepper

1. Pour drippings into measuring cup; spoon off 3 tablespoons fat and transfer to medium saucepan. Discard remaining fat. Set drippings aside.

2. Add flour to saucepan with fat; cook over medium heat 1 minute, stirring constantly.

3. Gradually stir in beef broth and reserved drippings. Cook over medium heat 10 minutes, stirring occasionally.

4. Stir in cream. Season to taste with salt and pepper.

Makes 8 to 10 servings

If you'd prefer a lighter gravy with a thinner consistency, simply omit the heavy whipping cream.

Cherry-Glazed Chicken

1 (2½- to 3-pound) broiler-fryer chicken, cut up (or 6 chicken
    breast halves, skinned and boned)

½ cup milk

½ cup all-purpose flour

1 teaspoon dried thyme

   Salt and pepper, to taste

1 to 2 tablespoons vegetable oil

1 (14.5-ounce) can unsweetened tart cherries

¼ cup granulated sugar

¼ cup brown sugar

1 teaspoon prepared yellow mustard

Rinse chicken; pat dry with paper towels. Pour milk into a shallow
container. In another container, combine flour, thyme, salt and
pepper. Dip chicken first in milk, then in flour mixture; coat evenly.
Heat oil in a large skillet. Add chicken; brown on all sides. Place
chicken in 13×9×2-inch baking dish. Bake, covered with aluminum
foil, in preheated 350°F oven 30 minutes.

Meanwhile, drain cherries, reserving ½ cup juice. Combine cherry
juice, granulated sugar and brown sugar in small saucepan; mix well.
Bring mixture to a boil over medium heat. Add mustard; mix well.
Cook 5 minutes, or until sauce is syrupy. Stir in cherries.

After chicken has cooked 30 minutes, remove baking dish from oven
and carefully remove foil cover. Spoon hot cherry mixture evenly over
chicken. Bake, uncovered, 15 minutes or until chicken is done. Serve
immediately.   *Makes 6 servings*

*Favorite recipe from **Cherry Marketing Institute***

Pork Roast with Corn Bread & Oyster Stuffing

1 (5- to 7-pound) pork loin roast*

2 tablespoons butter or margarine

½ cup chopped onion

½ cup chopped celery

2 cloves garlic, minced

½ teaspoon fennel seeds, crushed

1 teaspoon TABASCO® brand Pepper Sauce

½ teaspoon salt

2 cups packaged corn bread stuffing mix

1 (8-ounce) can oysters, undrained, chopped

*Have butcher crack backbone of pork loin roast.

Preheat oven to 325°F. Make a deep slit in back of each chop on pork loin. Melt butter in large saucepan; add onion, celery, garlic and fennel seeds. Cook 5 minutes or until vegetables are tender; stir in TABASCO® Sauce and salt. Add stuffing mix, oysters and oyster liquid; toss to mix well.

Stuff corn bread mixture into slits in pork. (Any leftover stuffing may be baked in covered baking dish during last 30 minutes of roasting.) Place meat in shallow roasting pan. Cook 30 to 35 minutes per pound or until meat thermometer inserted into pork roast registers 170°F. Remove to heated serving platter. Allow meat to stand 15 minutes before serving. *Makes 12 servings*

Festive Stuffed Fish

2 whole red snappers, about 2½ pounds each (or substitute any firm white fish), cleaned

Lemon and lime wedges

2 cloves garlic, minced

2 tablespoons Lucini Premium Select extra virgin olive oil

2 medium onions, finely chopped

1 cup seeded and chopped medium-hot pepper* (such as poblano, serrano, Anaheim or green bell variety)

1 cup chopped red bell pepper

8 ounces JARLSBERG or JARLSBERG LITE™ Cheese, shredded

12 tomatillos, thinly sliced, then chopped (about 2 cups)

1 cup dry white wine or unsweetened apple juice

Additional lemon and lime wedges

Chili peppers can sting and irritate the skin. Wear rubber gloves when handling peppers and do not touch your eyes. Wash hands after handling peppers.

Score flesh on each fish ¼ inch deep on the diagonal every 1½ inches. Insert lemon wedges, peel side out.

Cook garlic in olive oil in medium skillet over medium-high heat. Add onions and cook until translucent. Add peppers; cook 2 minutes. Place in large bowl; stir in cheese and tomatillos.

Stuff fish cavity with cheese mixture. Use kitchen string to tie each fish closed every 2 inches (3 or 4 ties). Set aside. Preheat oven to 375°F.

In same skillet, bring wine to a boil. Place fish in large glass or enamel baking dish. Pour hot wine over fish and cover tightly.

Bake 30 minutes or until fish is opaque. Transfer to serving platter and remove string. Garnish with additional lemon and lime wedges.

Makes 4 to 6 servings

Harvest Casserole

1 pound maple-flavored or regular pork sausage

2 acorn squash (about 2 pounds each)

1 cup cooked rice

½ cup dried cranberries

½ teaspoon salt

½ teaspoon ground cinnamon

½ teaspoon black pepper

1 can (10¾ ounces) condensed chicken broth, undiluted, divided

1. Preheat oven to 350°F. Grease 11×7-inch casserole; set aside.

2. Crumble sausage into skillet; cook and stir over medium-high heat until brown. Remove from heat and drain off drippings.

3. Meanwhile, pierce both squash in several places using sharp knife. Microwave on HIGH 8 minutes, turning over halfway through cooking time. When cool enough to handle, cut ½ inch off top and bottom of each squash. Cut each squash in half horizontally. Remove seeds and membrane. Place rings in prepared casserole.

4. Add rice, cranberries, salt, cinnamon and pepper to sausage. Add ¼ cup chicken broth to sausage to moisten. Spoon sausage mixture into squash rings. Pour remaining broth into casserole around rings.

5. Cover dish with foil. Bake 15 minutes. Remove foil and bake another 5 to 10 minutes or until squash is tender.

Makes 4 servings

Hint: This casserole can also be served as a side dish. Simply double the rice and omit the sausage.

Leg of Lamb with Apricot Stuffing

1 (6-ounce) package dried apricots, coarsely chopped

¼ cup apple juice

¼ cup wild rice, rinsed and drained

1½ cups chicken broth

½ cup long-grain rice

¼ cup chutney

¼ cup sliced green onions

2 teaspoons dried basil leaves

½ teaspoon lemon pepper

3 to 3½ pounds American leg of lamb, shank half, boned and butterflied

¼ teaspoon salt

¼ teaspoon ground black pepper

In bowl, combine apricots and apple juice; cover and let stand 20 minutes, stirring occasionally. In saucepan, combine wild rice and broth. Bring to a boil; reduce heat. Cover and simmer 40 minutes. Add long-grain rice. Cover and simmer 15 minutes more. Remove from heat. Let stand, covered, 5 minutes. Stir in apricot mixture, chutney (cut up any large chutney pieces), green onions, basil and lemon pepper.

Trim any fat from lamb. With boned side up, pound meat with meat mallet to even thickness, about 4 inches by 20 inches. Sprinkle lightly with salt and pepper. Spread rice mixture over meat. Roll up, starting with narrow end; tie securely. Place roast on end, seam side up, on rack in shallow roasting pan. Cover exposed rice mixture with small piece of foil. Roast at 325°F for 1¾ hours, or to medium doneness (150° to 160°F). Remove from oven. Let stand about 10 minutes. Remove strings; cut into wedges to serve.   *Makes 12 servings*

*Favorite recipe from **American Lamb Council***

Pork Roast with Dried Cranberries and Apricots

1 boneless center-cut pork loin roast (about 3½ pounds)

1½ cups cranberry-apple juice, divided

1 cup chardonnay or other dry white wine

1½ teaspoons ground ginger

1 teaspoon ground cardamom

2 tablespoons apricot preserves

¼ cup water

1 tablespoon plus 1 teaspoon cornstarch

½ cup dried cranberries

½ cup chopped dried apricots

2 tablespoons golden raisins

1. Place pork roast in large resealable food storage bag. Combine 1 cup cranberry-apple juice, wine, ginger and cardamom in medium bowl. Pour over roast, turning to coat. Seal bag. Marinate in refrigerator 4 hours or overnight, turning several times.

2. Preheat oven to 350°F. Remove roast from marinade; reserve marinade. Place roast in roasting pan. Pour marinade over roast. Bake, loosely covered with foil, 1 hour. Remove foil; continue baking 30 minutes or until internal temperature of roast reaches 165°F when tested with meat thermometer inserted into thickest part of roast. Transfer roast to cutting board; tent with foil. (Internal temperature will continue to rise 5°F to 10°F during stand time.)

3. Measure juices from pan. Add enough remaining cranberry-apple juice to equal 1½ cups. Combine juices and apricot preserves in small saucepan. Stir water into cornstarch in small bowl until smooth; stir into juice mixture. Bring to a boil over medium heat. Cook until thickened, stirring frequently. Add dried cranberries, apricots and raisins; cook 2 minutes. Remove from heat.

4. Cut roast into thin slices. Drizzle some sauce over roast; serve with remaining sauce.

Makes 10 servings

Spinach Stuffed Manicotti

1 package (10 ounces) frozen spinach

8 uncooked manicotti shells

1½ teaspoons olive oil

1 teaspoon dried rosemary

1 teaspoon dried sage

1 teaspoon dried oregano

1 teaspoon dried thyme

1 teaspoon chopped garlic

1½ cups chopped fresh tomatoes

½ cup ricotta cheese

½ cup fresh whole wheat bread crumbs

2 egg whites, lightly beaten

Yellow bell pepper rings and sage sprig (optional)

1. Cook spinach according to package directions. Place in colander to drain. Let stand until cool enough to handle. Squeeze spinach with hands to remove excess moisture. Set aside.

2. Cook pasta according to package directions; drain. Rinse under cold running water until cool enough to handle; drain.

3. Preheat oven to 350°F.

4. Heat oil in medium saucepan over medium heat. Cook and stir rosemary, sage, oregano, thyme and garlic in hot oil about 1 minute. *Do not let herbs turn brown.* Add tomatoes. Reduce heat to low. Simmer, uncovered, 10 minutes, stirring occasionally.

5. Combine spinach, cheese and bread crumbs in medium bowl. Fold in egg whites. Fill shells with spinach mixture.

6. Spread ⅓ of tomato mixture onto bottom of 13×9-inch baking dish. Arrange manicotti over tomato mixture. Pour remaining tomato mixture over top. Cover with foil. Bake 30 minutes or until bubbly. Garnish with yellow bell pepper rings and sage sprig.

Makes 4 servings

Maple-Glazed Ham

  1 **fully cooked bone-in ham (6 to 7 pounds)**
     Whole cloves
½ **cup maple syrup**
  2 **teaspoons cider vinegar**
  1 **teaspoon dry mustard**

1. Preheat oven to 350°F.

2. Cut skin off ham and trim off excess fat. Score top of ham in diamond design; stud with cloves. Place ham, fat side up, on rack in shallow roasting pan. Insert ovenproof meat thermometer into thickest part of ham, not touching bone.

3. Bake 1 hour 45 minutes to 2 hours (about 15 to 17 minutes per pound), or until meat thermometer registers 140°F.

4. Meanwhile, combine maple syrup, vinegar and mustard in small bowl. Remove ham from oven 30 minutes before baking is complete. Spoon maple glaze over top and sides of ham. Return to oven and continue baking.

5. Remove baked ham from oven; let stand 10 minutes. Transfer to serving platter. *Makes 8 to 10 servings*

If you happen to buy a ham that's not fully cooked, be sure to cook it to an internal temperature of 160°F.

Stuffed Cornish Game Hens

1 cup chicken broth

¾ cup uncooked couscous

1 tablespoon butter

¼ cup finely chopped shallots

¼ cup diced celery

¼ cup golden raisins

¼ cup chopped dates

¼ cup toasted pine nuts

1 teaspoon cumin

½ teaspoon salt

¼ teaspoon paprika

¼ teaspoon black pepper

4 Cornish game hens

2 tablespoons olive oil

Salt and black pepper

¾ cup orange marmalade, thinned with 2 tablespoons water

Orange slices (optional)

1. Bring broth to a boil in medium saucepan over medium heat; stir in couscous. Remove from heat; let stand, covered, 5 minutes. Transfer couscous to large bowl; fluff with fork. Set aside.

2. In same saucepan, melt butter over medium heat. Add shallots and celery; cook, stirring frequently, until shallots soften and begin to turn golden. Remove from heat; stir in raisins, dates, pine nuts, cumin, ½ teaspoon salt, paprika and ¼ teaspoon pepper.

3. Add shallot mixture to couscous; stir until well combined. Let cool 10 minutes.

4. Preheat oven to 450°F. Spray 11×7-inch baking pan with nonstick cooking spray. Stuff hens with couscous mixture; place on pan. Lightly coat outside of hens with olive oil; season with salt and pepper.

5. Roast hens 25 minutes. *Reduce oven temperature to 350°F.* Continue roasting about 25 minutes or until hens are golden brown and juices run clear when hens are pierced with a knife. Brush hens with marmalade during last 10 minutes of roasting. Transfer hens to large serving platter. Garnish with orange slices. *Makes 8 servings*

Apple Pecan Chicken Roll-Ups

½ **cup apple juice**

½ **cup UNCLE BEN'S® Instant Brown Rice**

½ **cup finely chopped unpeeled apple**

¼ **cup chopped pecans**

3 **tablespoons sliced green onions**

4 **boneless, skinless chicken breasts (about 1 pound)**

1 **tablespoon vegetable oil**

1. Heat oven to 400°F. In small saucepan, bring apple juice to a boil. Add rice; cover. Reduce heat. Simmer 8 to 10 minutes or until liquid is absorbed. Stir in apple, pecans and green onions. Remove from heat.

2. Flatten each chicken breast to about ¼-inch thickness by pounding between two pieces of waxed paper. Place ¼ of rice mixture on each chicken breast. Roll up, tucking in edges. Secure with toothpicks.

3. Heat oil in medium skillet over medium-high heat. Add chicken and cook 4 to 5 minutes or until lightly browned; place in shallow baking pan. Bake 20 to 25 minutes or until chicken is no longer pink in center. *Makes 4 servings*

Tip: For this recipe, choose an apple variety that will retain its shape when cooked, such as Granny Smith, Golden Delicious or Jonathan.

Cheese Ravioli with Pumpkin Sauce

Nonstick cooking spray
⅓ cup sliced green onions
1 to 2 cloves garlic, minced
½ teaspoon fennel seeds
1 cup evaporated milk
1 tablespoon all-purpose flour
¼ teaspoon salt
⅛ teaspoon black pepper
½ cup solid-pack pumpkin
2 packages (9 ounces each) uncooked refrigerated cheese ravioli
2 tablespoons grated Parmesan cheese

1. Spray medium nonstick saucepan with cooking spray; heat over medium heat until hot. Add onions, garlic and fennel seeds; cook and stir 3 minutes or until onions are tender.

2. Combine milk, flour, salt and pepper in small bowl until smooth; stir into saucepan. Bring to a boil over high heat; boil until thickened, stirring constantly. Stir in pumpkin; reduce heat to low.

3. Meanwhile, cook pasta according to package directions, omitting salt. Rinse. Drain. Divide ravioli evenly among 6 plates; top each with equal amount of pumpkin sauce. Sprinkle cheese evenly over top of each serving. Serve immediately. *Makes 6 servings*

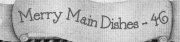

Country Chicken Pot Pie

  2 tablespoons butter

¾ pound boneless skinless chicken breasts, cut into 1-inch pieces

¾ teaspoon salt

  8 ounces fresh green beans, cut into 1-inch pieces (about 2 cups)

½ cup chopped red bell pepper

½ cup thinly sliced celery

  3 tablespoons all-purpose flour

½ cup chicken broth

½ cup half-and-half

  1 teaspoon dried thyme

½ teaspoon rubbed sage

  1 cup frozen pearl onions

½ cup frozen corn

   Pastry for single-crust 10-inch pie

1. Preheat oven to 425°F. Spray 10-inch deep-dish pie plate with nonstick cooking spray.

2. Melt butter in large deep skillet over medium-high heat. Add chicken; cook and stir 3 minutes or until no longer pink in center. Sprinkle with salt. Add green beans, bell pepper and celery; cook and stir 3 minutes.

3. Sprinkle flour evenly over chicken and vegetables; cook and stir 1 minute. Stir in broth, half-and-half, thyme and sage; bring to a boil over high heat. Reduce heat to low; simmer 3 minutes or until sauce is very thick. Stir in onions and corn. Return to a simmer; cook and stir 1 minute.

4. Transfer mixture to prepared pie plate. Place pie crust over chicken mixture; turn edge under and crimp to seal. Cut 4 slits in, or decorative pieces out of, pie crust to allow steam to escape. Bake 20 minutes or until crust is light golden brown and mixture is hot and bubbly. Let stand 5 minutes before serving. *Makes 6 servings*

Herb-Roasted Racks of Lamb

½ cup mango chutney, chopped

2 to 3 cloves garlic, minced

2 whole racks (6 ribs each) lamb loin chops (2½ to 3 pounds)

1 cup fresh French or Italian bread crumbs

1 tablespoon chopped fresh thyme *or* 1 teaspoon dried thyme

1 tablespoon chopped fresh rosemary *or* 1 teaspoon dried rosemary

1 tablespoon chopped fresh oregano *or* 1 teaspoon dried oregano

Additional fresh herb sprigs (optional)

Fresh mango slices (optional)

1. Preheat oven to 400°F. Combine chutney and garlic in small bowl; spread evenly over meaty side of lamb.

2. Combine remaining ingredients in separate small bowl; pat crumb mixture evenly over chutney mixture on chops.

3. Place lamb racks, crumb sides up, on rack in shallow roasting pan. Roast 30 to 35 minutes for medium or until internal temperature reaches 145°F when tested with meat thermometer inserted into thickest part of lamb, not touching bone.

4. Remove lamb to cutting board; tent with foil. Let stand 10 to 15 minutes before carving. (Internal temperature will continue to rise 5°F to 10°F during stand time.) Using large knife, slice between ribs into individual chops. Garnish with additional fresh herbs and mango slices. Serve immediately. *Makes 4 servings*

Holiday Hens with Sherry Gravy

- 4 teaspoons butter or margarine
- 2 teaspoons lemon juice
- 1 teaspoon Worcestershire sauce
- 3 packages (3 pounds each) PERDUE® Fresh Whole Cornish Hens (6 hens)
-   Salt and ground black pepper to taste
-   Scallion greens (optional)
- 6 sprigs fresh rosemary (optional)
- 3 tablespoons all-purpose flour
- 1 can (about 14 ounces) chicken broth
- ½ cup dry sherry

Preheat oven to 350°F. In large skillet over low heat, melt butter. Stir in lemon juice and Worcestershire sauce. Brush hens with butter mixture; sprinkle with salt and pepper. Tie legs together with kitchen string.

Place hens in large, shallow roasting pan. Roast 1 to 1¼ hours until skin is crisp and golden brown, juices run clear and no hint of pink remains when thigh is pierced. Remove to warm serving platter and discard string. Tie legs with scallion greens; garnish with rosemary.

To prepare sauce, stir flour into pan drippings. Cook over medium-low heat, 4 to 5 minutes until flour is brown, stirring constantly. Gradually whisk in chicken broth and sherry; cook 3 to 4 minutes longer, until gravy is smooth and thickened, stirring often. Strain gravy into a sauce dish and serve with hens. *Makes 8 to 12 servings*

Baked Holiday Ham with Cranberry-Wine Compote

2 teaspoons peanut oil
⅔ cup chopped onion
½ cup chopped celery
1 cup red wine
1 cup honey
½ cup sugar
1 package (12 ounces) fresh cranberries
1 fully-cooked smoked ham (10 pounds), skin removed
Whole cloves

1. For cranberry-wine compote, heat oil in large saucepan over medium-high heat until hot. Add onion and celery; cook and stir until tender. Stir in wine, honey and sugar; bring to a boil. Add cranberries; return to a boil. Reduce heat to low; cover and simmer 10 minutes. Cool completely.

2. Reserve 1 cup clear syrup from cranberry mixture. Transfer remaining cranberry mixture to small serving bowl; cover and refrigerate.

3. Preheat oven to 325°F. Score fat on ham in diamond design with sharp utility knife; stud with whole cloves. Place ham, fat side up, on rack in shallow roasting pan. Bake, uncovered, 1½ hours. Baste ham with reserved cranberry-wine syrup. Bake, basting with cranberry-wine syrup twice, 1 to 2 hours more or until meat thermometer inserted into thickest part of ham, not touching bone, registers 140°F.*

4. Remove ham from oven; let stand 10 minutes. Transfer to warm serving platter. Slice ham. Serve with chilled cranberry-wine compote.

Makes 16 to 20 servings

Total cooking time for ham should be 18 to 24 minutes per pound.

Heartland Crown Roast of Pork

Prep Time: 20 minutes
Cook Time: 1½ hours

  1 (8- to 9-pound) crown roast of pork
  1 pound ground pork, cooked, drained
  5 cups dry bread cubes
  1 can (14½ ounces) chicken broth
  1 cup walnut halves, toasted
  ½ cup chopped onion
  ½ cup chopped celery
  1 teaspoon salt
  ¼ teaspoon ground cinnamon
  ¼ teaspoon ground allspice
  ⅛ teaspoon pepper
  2 cups sliced fresh or thawed frozen rhubarb
  ½ cup sugar

Place roast in shallow pan. Roast at 350°F until temperature on meat thermometer reaches 155°F, about 1½ hours. Remove roast from oven. Let stand 10 minutes before slicing to serve.

Meanwhile, combine cooked ground pork, bread cubes, broth, walnuts, onion, celery and seasonings; mix well. Combine rhubarb and sugar in medium saucepan; bring to a boil. Pour over bread mixture; mix lightly. Spoon into buttered 2-quart casserole. Cover; bake at 350°F for 1½ hours. Serve with pork roast.

Makes 16 servings

Favorite recipe from **National Pork Board**

Vegetable Lasagna

Tomato-Basil Sauce (recipe follows)

2 **tablespoons olive oil**

4 **medium carrots, thinly sliced**

3 **medium zucchini, thinly sliced**

6 **ounces spinach leaves, washed, stemmed and torn into bite-size pieces**

¼ **teaspoon salt**

¼ **teaspoon black pepper**

1 **egg**

3 **cups ricotta cheese**

½ **cup plus 2 tablespoons grated Parmesan cheese, divided**

12 **uncooked lasagna noodles**

1½ **cups (6 ounces) shredded mozzarella cheese**

1½ **cups (6 ounces) shredded Monterey Jack cheese**

½ **cup water**

Belgian endive leaves, Bibb lettuce leaves and fresh basil sprigs (optional)

1. Prepare Tomato-Basil Sauce.

2. Heat oil in large skillet over medium heat until hot. Add carrots; cook and stir 4 minutes. Add zucchini; cook and stir 8 minutes or until crisp-tender. Add spinach; cook and stir 1 minute or until spinach is wilted. Stir in salt and pepper.

3. Preheat oven to 350°F. Beat egg in medium bowl. Stir in ricotta and ½ cup Parmesan cheese.

4. Spread 1 cup Tomato-Basil Sauce in bottom of 13×9-inch baking pan; top with 4 uncooked lasagna noodles. Spread ⅓ of ricotta cheese mixture over noodles.

5. Spoon ⅓ of vegetable mixture over cheese. Top with 1 cup Tomato-Basil Sauce. Sprinkle with ½ cup each mozzarella and Monterey Jack cheeses.

6. Repeat layers twice, beginning with noodles and ending with mozzarella and Monterey Jack cheeses. Sprinkle with remaining 2 tablespoons Parmesan cheese.

7. Carefully pour water around sides of pan. Cover pan tightly with foil.

8. Bake lasagna 1 hour or until bubbly. Remove from oven. Uncover; let stand 10 to 15 minutes. Cut into squares. Garnish with greens and fresh herbs. *Makes 8 servings*

Tomato-Basil Sauce

2 cans (28 ounces each) plum tomatoes

1 teaspoon olive oil

1 medium onion, chopped

3 cloves garlic, minced

1 tablespoon sugar

1 tablespoon dried basil

¼ teaspoon salt

¼ teaspoon black pepper

1. Drain tomatoes, reserving ½ cup juice. Seed and chop tomatoes.

2. Heat oil in large skillet over medium heat until hot. Add onion and garlic; cook and stir 5 minutes or until tender.

3. Stir in tomatoes, reserved juice, sugar, basil, salt and pepper. Bring to a boil over high heat.

4. Reduce heat to low. Simmer, uncovered, 25 to 30 minutes or until most of juices have evaporated. *Makes 4 cups sauce*

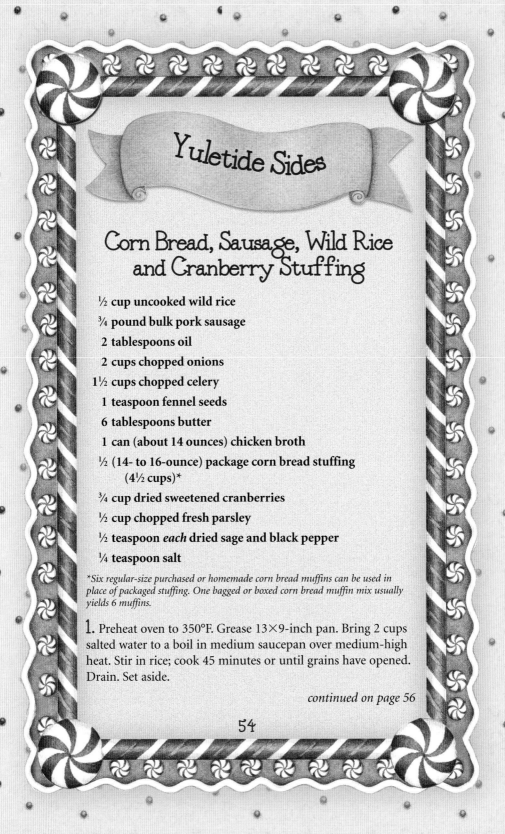

Corn Bread, Sausage, Wild Rice and Cranberry Stuffing

½ cup uncooked wild rice

¾ pound bulk pork sausage

2 tablespoons oil

2 cups chopped onions

1½ cups chopped celery

1 teaspoon fennel seeds

6 tablespoons butter

1 can (about 14 ounces) chicken broth

½ (14- to 16-ounce) package corn bread stuffing (4½ cups)*

¾ cup dried sweetened cranberries

½ cup chopped fresh parsley

½ teaspoon *each* dried sage and black pepper

¼ teaspoon salt

Six regular-size purchased or homemade corn bread muffins can be used in place of packaged stuffing. One bagged or boxed corn bread muffin mix usually yields 6 muffins.

1. Preheat oven to 350°F. Grease 13×9-inch pan. Bring 2 cups salted water to a boil in medium saucepan over medium-high heat. Stir in rice; cook 45 minutes or until grains have opened. Drain. Set aside.

continued on page 56

54

Corn Bread, Sausage, Wild Rice and Cranberry Stuffing

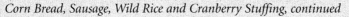

Corn Bread, Sausage, Wild Rice and Cranberry Stuffing, continued

2. Cook sausage in large nonstick skillet over medium-high heat 10 minutes or until cooked through, stirring to break up meat. Transfer to large bowl.

3. Heat oil in same skillet over medium-high heat. Add onions, celery and fennel seeds; cook 6 to 8 minutes or until softened, stirring occasionally. Remove to bowl with sausage.

4. Add butter and chicken broth to same skillet; heat over high heat until butter melts. Remove from heat. Add corn bread; toss to mix.

5. To the sausage mixture, add reserved rice, corn bread mixture, cranberries, parsley, sage, pepper and salt; toss to mix. Transfer to prepared pan. Bake, covered, 30 minutes. Uncover; bake 30 minutes more or until top is crisped. *Makes 8 servings*

Green Bean Casserole

Prep Time: 5 minutes
Cook Time: 35 minutes

    1 can (10¾ ounces) **condensed cream of mushroom soup**

    ¾ cup **milk**

    ⅛ teaspoon **ground black pepper**

    2 packages (9 ounces each) **frozen cut green beans, thawed and drained** *or* 2 cans (14½ ounces each) **cut green beans, drained**

    1⅓ cups *French's®* **French Fried Onions, divided**

Preheat oven to 350°F. Combine soup, milk and ground pepper in 1½-quart casserole; stir until well blended. Stir in beans and ⅔ *cup* French Fried Onions. Bake, uncovered, 30 minutes or until hot. Stir; sprinkle with remaining ⅔ *cup* onions. Bake 5 minutes or until onions are golden. *Makes 6 servings*

Microwave Directions: Prepare green bean mixture as above. Pour into 1½-quart microwavable casserole. Cover loosely with plastic wrap. Microwave on HIGH 8 to 10 minutes or until heated through, stirring halfway through cooking time. Uncover; sprinkle with remaining onions. Cook 1 minute or until onions are golden. Let stand 5 minutes.

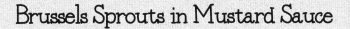

Brussels Sprouts in Mustard Sauce

1½ **pounds fresh brussels sprouts***

  1 **tablespoon butter or margarine**

⅓ **cup chopped shallots or onion**

⅓ **cup half-and-half**

  1 **tablespoon plus 1½ teaspoons Dijon mustard or Dusseldorf mustard**

½ **teaspoon dried tarragon**

¼ **teaspoon salt**

⅛ **teaspoon black pepper or ground nutmeg**

1½ **tablespoons grated Parmesan cheese (optional)**

*Or, substitute 2 (10-ounce) packages frozen brussels sprouts. Cook according to package directions; drain and rinse as directed.

1. Cut stem from each brussels sprout and pull off outer bruised leaves. Cut an "X" deep into stem end of each brussels sprout. If some brussels sprouts are larger than others, cut large brussels sprouts lengthwise into halves.

2. Bring 2 quarts salted water to a boil in large saucepan. Add brussels sprouts; return to a boil. Boil, uncovered, 7 to 10 minutes or until almost tender when pierced with fork. Drain in colander. Rinse under cold water; drain thoroughly.

3. Melt butter in same saucepan over medium heat. Add shallots; cook 3 minutes, stirring occasionally.

4. Add half-and-half, mustard, tarragon, salt and pepper; simmer 1 minute or until thickened.

5. Add drained brussels sprouts; heat about 1 minute or until heated through, tossing gently with sauce.

6. Sprinkle with cheese, if desired.   *Makes 6 to 8 servings*

Basic Turkey Gravy

Reserved neck, heart and gizzard from a Turkey giblets package
1 medium carrot, thickly sliced
1 medium onion, thickly sliced
1 medium stalk celery, thickly sliced
1 teaspoon salt, divided
1 turkey liver
3 tablespoons fat from poultry drippings
3 tablespoons all-purpose flour
Black pepper (to taste)

1. In 3-quart saucepan, over high heat, place neck, heart, gizzard, vegetables and ½ teaspoon salt in enough cold water to cover. Heat to boiling. Reduce heat to low; cover and simmer 45 minutes.

2. Add liver and simmer 15 minutes. Strain broth into large bowl; cover and reserve giblet broth in refrigerator.

3. To make gravy, remove cooked turkey and roasting rack from roasting pan. Strain poultry drippings into 4-cup measuring cup.

4. Add 1 cup giblet broth to roasting pan and stir until crusty brown bits are loosened. Pour liquid into cup with drippings. Let mixture stand until fat rises to top.

5. Over medium heat, spoon 3 tablespoons fat from poultry drippings into 2-quart saucepan. Whisk flour and remaining ½ teaspoon salt into fat; cook and stir until flour turns golden.

6. Meanwhile, skim and discard any fat remaining on top of poultry drippings. Add remaining giblet broth and enough water to poultry drippings to equal 3½ cups.

7. Gradually whisk in warm poultry drippings-broth mixture. Cook and stir until gravy boils and thickens slightly.

Makes about 4 cups

Giblet Gravy: Pull cooked meat from the neck and discard bones. Coarsely chop neck meat and cooked giblets. Cover and reserve in refrigerator. Stir reserved giblets and neck meat into prepared Basic Turkey Gravy. Season with salt and black pepper. Heat to a simmer.

Sherry Gravy: Add ⅓ cup sherry to prepared Basic Turkey Gravy. Season with salt and black pepper. Heat to a simmer.

Mushroom Gravy: Clean and thinly slice ½ pound button mushrooms. Melt 1½ tablespoons butter in large skillet over high heat. Add sliced mushrooms and sauté until mushrooms are tender and all liquid has evaporated, about 3 to 4 minutes. Cover and reserve. Add mushrooms to prepared Basic Turkey Gravy and heat to a simmer. Season with salt and black pepper.

*Favorite recipe from **National Turkey Federation***

Applesauce Cranberry Mold

- 2 **envelopes unflavored gelatin**
- ½ **cup orange or cranberry juice**
- ½ **cup boiling water**
- 1 **can or jar (16 ounces) whole-berry cranberry sauce**
- 1 **cup applesauce**
- 1 **apple, cored and cut up**
- 1 **cup diced celery**
- ½ **cup chopped walnuts**
- 1 **orange, peeled and diced**
- 2 **tablespoons grated orange peel**

Soften gelatin in juice. Add boiling water and stir to dissolve; cool. Mix all other ingredients; add to gelatin mixture. Pour into greased 2-quart mold and refrigerate several hours.   *Makes 6 to 8 servings*

*Favorite recipe from **New York Apple Association, Inc.***

Golden Corn Pudding

Prep Time: 10 minutes
Bake Time: 35 minutes

- 2 tablespoons butter or margarine
- 3 tablespoons all-purpose flour
- 1 can (14¾ ounces) DEL MONTE® Cream Style Golden Sweet Corn
- ¼ cup yellow cornmeal
- 2 eggs, separated
- 1 package (3 ounces) cream cheese, softened
- 1 can (8¾ ounces) DEL MONTE Whole Kernel Golden Sweet Corn, drained

1. Preheat oven to 350°F.

2. Melt butter in medium saucepan. Add flour and stir until smooth. Blend in cream style corn and cornmeal. Bring to a boil over medium heat, stirring constantly.

3. Place egg yolks in small bowl; stir in ½ cup hot mixture. Pour mixture back into saucepan. Add cream cheese and whole kernel corn.

4. Place egg whites in clean narrow bowl and beat until stiff peaks form. With rubber spatula, gently fold egg whites into corn mixture.

5. Pour mixture into 1½-quart straight-sided baking dish. Bake 30 to 35 minutes or until lightly browned.   *Makes 4 to 6 servings*

Tip: Pudding can be prepared up to 3 hours ahead of serving time. Cover and refrigerate until about 30 minutes before baking.

Barley and Wild Rice Pilaf

½ cup uncooked wild rice

2 tablespoons olive oil, divided

1 medium onion, chopped

1 cup uncooked pearl barley

3 cloves garlic, minced

4 cups chicken broth

1 large red bell pepper, cut into ¼-inch pieces

3 ounces fresh mushrooms, thinly sliced

½ cup frozen green peas, thawed

½ cup shredded carrot

1 teaspoon dried oregano *or* 1 tablespoon chopped fresh oregano

1. Rinse rice in fine strainer under cold running water. Drain; set aside.

2. Heat 1 tablespoon oil in 3-quart saucepan over medium-high heat. Add onion; cook and stir about 10 minutes or until tender. Add barley, rice and garlic; cook and stir over medium heat 1 minute.

3. Stir in chicken broth. Bring to a boil over medium-high heat. Reduce heat to low; simmer, covered, about 1 hour or until barley and rice are tender.

4. Heat remaining 1 tablespoon oil in large skillet over medium-high heat. Add bell pepper, mushrooms, peas, carrot and oregano; cook and stir 5 to 6 minutes or until vegetables are tender.

5. Stir bell pepper mixture into rice mixture. *Makes 8 servings*

Vegetable Tart

Pastry Dough (recipe follows)

Olive oil-flavored nonstick cooking spray

1 small sweet potato

1 tablespoon olive or vegetable oil

1 cup sliced mushrooms

½ cup thinly sliced leeks

1 medium zucchini, sliced

1 parsnip, sliced

1 medium red bell pepper, cut into 1-inch pieces

8 to 10 cloves garlic, minced

1 teaspoon dried basil

½ teaspoon dried rosemary

½ teaspoon salt

Black pepper (optional)

2 to 4 tablespoons grated Parmesan cheese

1 egg white, beaten

1. Preheat oven to 400°F. Prepare Pastry Dough. While dough is resting, begin preparing vegetables for tart.

2. Spray nonstick baking sheet with cooking spray. Slice sweet potato into ¼-inch-thick slices. Place on prepared baking sheet; spray tops of slices with cooking spray. Bake 15 to 20 minutes or until slices are tender, turning once.

3. Heat oil in large skillet over medium heat until hot. Add mushrooms, leeks, zucchini, parsnip, bell pepper, garlic, basil and rosemary; cook and stir 8 to 10 minutes or until vegetables are tender. Season to taste with salt and black pepper, if desired.

4. Roll out Pastry Dough on lightly floured surface to a 14-inch round; place on cookie sheet or large pizza pan. Place sweet potato slices evenly over crust, leaving a 2½-inch border around edge. Spoon

vegetable mixture evenly over potatoes. Sprinkle with cheese. Fold edge of dough over edge of vegetable mixture, pleating dough, as necessary, to fit. Brush edge of dough with egg white.

5. Bake 25 minutes or until pastry is golden brown. Cut into wedges; serve warm.   *Makes 16 servings*

Pastry Dough

 1 teaspoon active dry yeast

⅓ cup warm water (115°F)

 1 egg, beaten

 3 tablespoons fat-free sour cream

1¼ cups all-purpose flour

¼ cup whole wheat flour

¼ teaspoon salt

1. Sprinkle yeast over warm water in medium bowl; stir until yeast is dissolved. Let stand 5 minutes or until mixture is bubbly.

2. Add egg and sour cream to bowl, mixing until smooth. Stir in flours and salt, making soft dough.

3. Knead dough on lightly floured surface 1 to 2 minutes or until smooth. Shape dough into ball; place in large bowl sprayed with olive oil-flavored nonstick cooking spray. Turn dough over to grease top. Cover bowl with clean kitchen towel; let rest in warm place 20 minutes.   *Makes pastry for 1 tart*

Get creative! Try some of your other favorite vegetable combinations in place of the ones given in this recipe.

Festive Cranberry Mold

½ cup water

1 package (6 ounces) raspberry-flavored gelatin

1 can (8 ounces) jellied cranberry sauce

1⅔ cups cranberry juice cocktail

1 cup sliced bananas (optional)

½ cup walnuts, toasted (optional)

1. Bring water to a boil in medium saucepan over medium-high heat. Add gelatin and stir until dissolved. Fold in cranberry sauce. Reduce heat to medium; cook until sauce is melted. Stir in cranberry juice cocktail.

2. Refrigerate mixture until slightly thickened. Fold in banana slices and walnuts, if desired. Pour mixture into 4-cup mold; cover and refrigerate until gelatin is set.   *Makes 8 servings*

Holiday Harvest Rice

2 tablespoons margarine

1½ cups MAHATMA®, CAROLINA®, RIVER® or WATER MAID® rice

½ teaspoon salt

2 cups unsweetened apple juice

1 cup cranberry juice

2 tablespoons fresh lemon juice

1 tablespoon chopped raisins

2 teaspoons light brown sugar

½ teaspoon ground cinnamon

2 small tart apples, peeled, cored and chopped

½ cup chopped green onions

In saucepan, over medium heat, melt margarine. Stir in rice and salt, stirring to coat rice. Add juices, raisins, sugar and cinnamon. Bring to a boil. Cover and simmer 20 minutes. Stir in apples and green onions.
Makes 6 to 8 servings

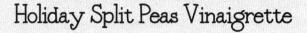

Holiday Split Peas Vinaigrette

4 cups green or yellow split peas, washed

2 quarts water

3 pounds cooked smoked sausage, sliced

12 medium (4 pounds) onions, finely chopped and steamed or sautéed

2 cups olive oil

¾ cup vinegar

1½ cups chopped fresh parsley

⅓ cup German hot or coarse mustard

Sugar to taste

Salt and white pepper to taste

12 medium (4 pounds) tomatoes or red bell peppers, coarsely chopped and sautéed

1. Combine split peas and water in stockpot; bring to a boil. Reduce heat and simmer 20 minutes or until peas are tender.

2. Remove from heat; drain, if necessary. Stir in sausage and onions. Keep warm.

3. Blend together oil, vinegar, parsley, mustard, sugar, salt and pepper.

4. Pour oil mixture over split pea mixture; blend.

5. Gently stir in tomatoes. Serve immediately as warm salad or cassoulet. Cover and refrigerate several hours for chilled salad.

Makes 24 (1½-cup) servings

*Favorite recipe from **USA Dry Pea & Lentil Council***

Succotash

1 tablespoon CRISCO® Pure Canola Oil*

½ cup chopped red bell pepper

4 to 6 chopped scallions, white and green parts, separated

1 (10-ounce) package frozen baby lima beans, defrosted

1 (10-ounce) package frozen corn kernels, defrosted

¼ cup water

1 teaspoon salt

Black pepper to taste

*Or use your favorite Crisco Oil.

Heat CRISCO Pure Canola Oil in a large skillet or saucepan over medium heat. Add red pepper and cook until just tender. Add white parts of scallions and stir. Add lima beans, corn, water, salt and pepper; stir well to combine.

Cover and cook about 5 minutes until vegetables are cooked to your liking. Stir in green parts of the scallions. Taste and add salt and pepper if needed. *Makes 4 to 6 servings*

Sour Cream Garlic Mashed Potatoes

2 pounds red potatoes, peeled* and cut into 1-inch chunks

6 cloves garlic, peeled

¼ cup (½ stick) butter

1 cup sour cream

1 teaspoon salt

½ teaspoon white pepper

*For more texture, leave the potatoes unpeeled.

Place potatoes and garlic cloves in large saucepan; cover with water. Bring to a boil over high heat. Reduce heat; simmer about 20 minutes or until potatoes are tender. Drain well in colander; return to saucepan. Add butter; mash potatoes. Stir in sour cream, salt and white pepper. *Makes 8 to 10 servings*

Sweet Potato Soufflé

1¼ **pounds (about 3 medium) sweet potatoes**
  1 **tablespoon butter**
  ¾ **cup heavy cream**
  1 **teaspoon salt**
  ¼ **teaspoon white pepper**
  ¼ **teaspoon ground nutmeg**
  5 **egg whites**
   Boiling water

1. Place unpeeled potatoes in medium saucepan; cover with water. Bring to a boil. Reduce heat; cover. Boil 20 minutes or until fork-tender. Drain well and cool to room temperature.

2. Preheat oven to 375°F. Generously butter 1½-quart soufflé dish.

3. Peel potatoes and mash with cream, salt, white pepper and nutmeg; beat with wooden spoon or electric mixer until smooth.

4. Beat egg whites with electric mixer until stiff peaks form. Gently but thoroughly fold egg whites into potato mixture until completely incorporated.

5. Pour into prepared soufflé dish. Place soufflé dish in 13×9-inch baking pan and place in oven. Pour enough boiling water into baking pan to come 1 inch up side of soufflé dish. Bake for 1 hour and 10 minutes or until knife inserted in center comes out clean.

Makes 8 servings

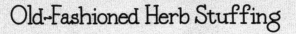

Old-Fashioned Herb Stuffing

6 slices (8 ounces) whole wheat, rye or white bread (or combination), cut into ½-inch cubes

1 tablespoon butter or margarine

1 cup chopped onion

½ cup thinly sliced celery

½ cup thinly sliced carrot

1 cup chicken broth

1 tablespoon chopped fresh thyme *or* 1 teaspoon dried thyme

1 tablespoon chopped fresh sage *or* 1 teaspoon dried sage

½ teaspoon paprika

¼ teaspoon black pepper

1. Preheat oven to 350°F. Place bread cubes on baking sheet; bake 10 minutes or until dry.

2. Melt butter in large saucepan over medium heat. Add onion, celery and carrot; cover and cook 10 minutes or until vegetables are tender.

3. Add broth, thyme, sage, paprika and pepper to saucepan; bring to a simmer. Stir in bread pieces; mix well. Remove pan from heat; set aside.

4. Coat 1½-quart baking dish with nonstick cooking spray. Spoon stuffing into dish. Cover and bake 25 to 30 minutes or until heated through.
Makes 4 servings

Nutty Vegetable Pilaf

1 tablespoon vegetable oil

2 cups coarsely chopped broccoli

2 medium carrots, julienned

1 medium onion, chopped

1 cup sliced fresh mushrooms

2 cloves garlic, minced

½ teaspoon dried thyme leaves

½ teaspoon dried basil leaves

½ teaspoon salt

¼ teaspoon ground black pepper

3 cups cooked brown rice (cooked in low-sodium chicken broth*)

½ cup chopped pecans, toasted**

½ cup grated Parmesan cheese (optional)

*For a vegetarian dish, cook brown rice in vegetable broth.

**To toast pecans, place on baking sheet; bake 5 to 7 minutes in 350°F oven, or until nuts are just beginning to darken and are fragrant.

Heat oil in large skillet over medium-high heat until hot. Add broccoli, carrots and onion. Cook and stir 5 to 7 minutes or until broccoli and carrots are tender and onion is beginning to brown. Add mushrooms, garlic, thyme, basil, salt and pepper. Cook and stir 2 to 3 minutes or until mushrooms are tender. Add rice and pecans; cook 1 to 2 minutes, stirring, until well blended and thoroughly heated. Just before serving sprinkle with cheese, if desired.

Makes 6 servings

Favorite recipe from USA Rice

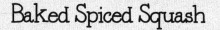

Baked Spiced Squash

Prep Time: 5 minutes
Cook Time: 25 to 35 minutes

> 2 boxes (10 ounces each) BIRDS EYE® frozen Cooked Winter
>   Squash, thawed
> 2 egg whites, lightly beaten
> ¼ cup brown sugar
> 2 teaspoons butter or margarine, melted
> 1 teaspoon ground cinnamon
> ½ cup herbed croutons, coarsely crushed

• Preheat oven to 400°F. Combine squash, egg whites, sugar, butter and cinnamon; mix well.

• Pour into 1-quart baking dish sprayed with nonstick cooking spray.

• Bake 20 to 25 minutes or until center is set.

• Remove from oven; sprinkle crushed croutons on top. Bake 5 to 7 minutes longer or until croutons are browned.

Makes 6 to 8 servings

This side dish looks particularly festive
at Thanksgiving gatherings. Use an
8-inch square baking pan, and garnish
with a few squash or carrot shavings.

Potatoes au Gratin

2 medium unpeeled baking potatoes (about 1 pound)

1 cup (4 ounces) shredded Cheddar cheese

½ cup (2 ounces) shredded Swiss cheese

1 tablespoon butter or margarine

1 tablespoon plus 1½ teaspoons all-purpose flour

1 cup milk

1 tablespoon Dijon mustard

⅛ teaspoon salt

⅛ teaspoon black pepper

1. Preheat oven to 400°F. Spray 2 (18×18-inch) sheets heavy-duty foil with nonstick cooking spray.

2. Cut potatoes into thin slices. Arrange ¼ of potato slices on each sheet of foil. Top with half the cheeses. Repeat layers with remaining potatoes and cheeses. Fold foil up around potatoes.

3. Melt butter in medium saucepan over medium heat. Stir in flour; cook 1 minute. Stir in milk, mustard, salt and pepper; bring to a boil. Reduce heat and cook, stirring constantly, until mixture thickens. Carefully pour milk mixture into packets.

4. Double fold sides and ends of foil to seal packets, leaving headspace for heat circulation. Place packets on baking sheet.

5. Bake 25 minutes. Remove packets from oven. Carefully open tops of packets. Return to oven and bake 10 minutes more or until potatoes are tender and tops are brown. Remove from oven and let stand 10 minutes before serving.   *Makes 2 to 3 servings*

Fresh Cranberry Apple Sauce

Prep Time: 15 minutes
Chill Time: 120 minutes

- 1 package (12 ounces) fresh cranberries
- 1 large Red Delicious or Cortland apple, peeled and diced
- 1¼ cups sugar
- ¾ cup orange juice
- ¼ cup KARO® Light or Dark Corn Syrup

Place cranberries in sieve; rinse with cool running water. Drain well. Discard any soft or discolored berries.

In 2½- to 3-quart saucepan, combine cranberries, diced apple, sugar, orange juice and Karo. Stirring frequently, bring to a boil over medium-high heat.

Reduce heat and simmer, stirring occasionally, 5 to 8 minutes or until slightly thickened.

Refrigerate until cool, about 2 hours, stirring occasionally.

Makes 3 cups

Honey-Glazed Carrots

- 3 cups sliced carrots
- 6 tablespoons honey
- 2 tablespoons butter or margarine
- 2 tablespoons chopped fresh parsley
- 1½ teaspoons Dijon mustard (optional)

Bring 2 inches of salted water to a boil in medium saucepan over high heat. Add carrots and return to a boil. Reduce heat to medium. Cover and cook 8 to 12 minutes or until carrots are crisp-tender. Drain carrots; return to saucepan. Stir in honey, butter, parsley and mustard, if desired. Cook and stir over low heat until carrots are glazed.

Makes 6 servings

*Favorite recipe from **National Honey Board***

Roasted Fall Root Vegetables

½ **pound potatoes**

½ **pound sweet potatoes**

½ **pound carrots**

½ **pound beets**

1 **cup chopped onion**

3 to 4 **cloves garlic, minced**

¼ **cup CRISCO® Pure Canola Oil***

½ **teaspoon dried thyme**

Salt and pepper to taste

*Or use your favorite Crisco Oil.

Heat oven to 350°F.

Peel and cut potatoes, sweet potatoes, carrots and beets into ½-inch cubes. Place in large bowl; add remaining ingredients and salt and pepper to taste. Toss to mix well.

Place mixture on large ungreased baking sheet; bake for about 25 to 30 minutes or until vegetables can be easily pierced with fork.

Makes 4 to 6 servings

Note: Any variety of root vegetables, such as turnips, parsnips, rutabagas, potatoes, carrots, sweet potatoes, yams or beets, can be used in any combination. Use more or less as desired.

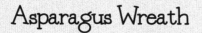

Asparagus Wreath

1 pound fresh asparagus, ends trimmed

1 tablespoon butter or margarine

1 teaspoon lemon juice

6 thin slices pepperoni, finely chopped

¼ cup seasoned dry bread crumbs

    Pimiento strips for garnish

1. Peel asparagus stalks, if desired. Steam asparagus in large covered saucepan 5 to 8 minutes or until crisp-tender.

2. Arrange asparagus in wreath shape on warm, round serving platter.

3. Heat butter and lemon juice in small saucepan until butter is melted; pour over asparagus. Combine chopped pepperoni and bread crumbs in small bowl; sprinkle over asparagus. Garnish with pimiento strips, if desired. *Makes 4 servings*

Simplest-Ever Holiday Gravy

1 tablespoon olive oil

1 tablespoon butter

3 tablespoons all-purpose flour

2 cups hot chicken broth

    Pinch of garlic powder

    Salt and black pepper

1. Heat olive oil in medium saucepan over high heat. Add butter. When butter is melted and foaming, whisk in flour. Whisk constantly about 30 seconds to 1 minute. Whisk in hot broth, stirring constantly until simmering and thickened, about 3 minutes.

2. Remove from heat. Season with garlic powder, salt and pepper. Gravy will thicken as it cools. *Makes 2 cups gravy*

Baked Acorn Squash with Apples and Raisins

2 medium acorn squash (about 2¼ pounds)

⅓ cup pancake syrup

1 Granny Smith apple, peeled, cored and coarsely chopped

¼ cup seedless raisins

⅛ teaspoon ground nutmeg

1½ teaspoons cornstarch

2 tablespoons water

1. Preheat oven to 400°F. Cut squash into halves with large knife. Scoop out and discard seeds. Place squash, cut side down, in 13×9-inch baking dish. Add 1 cup water to baking dish; bake 35 to 45 minutes or until fork-tender. Turn squash cut-side-up.

2. Meanwhile, heat syrup in medium saucepan over medium heat. Add apple, raisins and nutmeg; cook and stir about 8 minutes or until apple is almost crisp-tender.

3. Combine cornstarch and 2 tablespoons water in small cup until smooth; stir into saucepan. Cook and stir over medium-high heat until mixture boils and thickens. Cook and stir 2 minutes more.

4. Divide mixture evenly among squash halves. Return squash to oven; bake 10 minutes more or until heated through.

Makes 4 servings

Holiday Vegetable Bake

Prep Time: 5 minutes
Cook Time: 10 minutes

> 1 package (16 ounces) frozen vegetable combination
> 1 can (10¾ ounces) condensed cream of broccoli soup
> ⅓ cup milk
> 1⅓ cups *French's*® French Fried Onions, divided

Microwave Directions

Combine vegetables, soup, milk and ⅔ *cup* French Fried Onions in 2-quart microwavable casserole. Microwave,* uncovered, on HIGH 10 to 12 minutes or until vegetables are crisp-tender, stirring halfway through cooking time. Sprinkle with remaining ⅔ *cup* onions. Microwave 1 minute or until onions are golden.

Makes 4 to 6 servings

*Or, bake in preheated 375°F oven 30 to 35 minutes.

Cranberry Pear Sauce

> 1 package (12 ounces) fresh or frozen cranberries
> 1 cup packed light brown sugar
> ½ cup white grape juice or apple cider
> ¼ teaspoon ground allspice
> 1 large ripe pear, peeled and diced

Combine cranberries, brown sugar, grape juice and allspice in medium saucepan. Bring to a boil over high heat. Reduce heat; simmer, uncovered, 10 minutes or until thickened, stirring frequently. Stir in pear; cook 3 minutes if pear is not ripe, 1 minute if pear is ripe. Remove from heat; cool completely. Cover; chill at least 2 hours or up to 24 hours before serving.

Makes 8 to 10 servings

Holiday Fruit Salad

3 packages (4 servings each) strawberry flavor gelatin

3 cups boiling water

2 ripe DOLE® Bananas

1 package (16 ounces) DOLE® Fresh Frozen Strawberries

1 can (20 ounces) DOLE® Crushed Pineapple

1 package (8 ounces) cream cheese, softened

1 cup dairy sour cream or plain yogurt

¼ cup sugar

Crisp DOLE® Lettuce leaves

• In large bowl, dissolve gelatin in boiling water. Slice bananas into gelatin mixture. Add frozen strawberries and undrained crushed pineapple. Reserve half of the mixture at room temperature. Pour remaining mixture into 13×9-inch pan. Refrigerate 1 hour or until firm.

• In mixer bowl, beat cream cheese with sour cream and sugar; spread over chilled layer. Gently spoon reserved gelatin mixture on top. Refrigerate until firm, about 2 hours.

• Cut into squares; serve on lettuce-lined salad plates. Garnish with additional pineapple and mint leaves, if desired.

Makes 12 servings

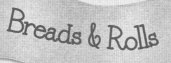

Cranberry-Raisin Nut Bread

1½ cups all-purpose flour

¾ cup packed light brown sugar

1½ teaspoons baking powder

½ teaspoon baking soda

½ teaspoon ground cinnamon

½ teaspoon ground nutmeg

1 cup coarsely chopped fresh or frozen cranberries

½ cup golden raisins

½ cup coarsely chopped pecans

1 tablespoon grated orange peel

2 eggs

¾ cup milk

3 tablespoons butter, melted

1 teaspoon vanilla

Cranberry-Orange Spread (page 80)

1. Preheat oven to 350°F. Grease 8½×4½-inch loaf pan.

2. Combine flour, brown sugar, baking powder, baking soda, cinnamon and nutmeg in large bowl. Stir in cranberries, raisins, pecans and orange peel. Mix eggs, milk, butter and vanilla in small bowl until combined; stir into flour mixture just until moistened. Spoon into prepared pan.

continued on page 80

Cranberry-Raisin Nut Bread

Cranberry-Raisin Nut Bread, continued

3. Bake 55 to 60 minutes or until toothpick inserted into center comes out clean. Cool in pan 15 minutes. Remove from pan to wire rack; cool completely. Store tightly wrapped in plastic wrap at room temperature. Serve with Cranberry-Orange Spread.   *Makes 1 loaf*

Cranberry-Orange Spread

1 package (8 ounces) cream cheese, softened

1 package (3 ounces) cream cheese, softened

1 container (12 ounces) cranberry-orange sauce

¾ cup chopped pecans

Combine cream cheese and cranberry-orange sauce in small bowl; stir until blended. Stir in pecans. Store in refrigerator.

Makes about 3 cups spread

Pumpkin Bread

1 package (about 18 ounces) yellow cake mix

1 can (16 ounces) solid-pack pumpkin

4 eggs

⅓ cup GRANDMA'S® Molasses

1 teaspoon cinnamon

1 teaspoon nutmeg

⅓ cup chopped nuts (optional)

⅓ cup raisins (optional)

Preheat oven to 350°F. Grease two 9×5-inch loaf pans.

Combine all ingredients in large bowl and mix well. Beat with electric mixer at medium speed 2 minutes. Pour into prepared pans. Bake 60 minutes or until toothpick inserted into centers comes out clean.   *Makes 2 loaves*

Hint: Serve with cream cheese or preserves, or top with cream cheese frosting or ice cream.

Apple Country® Bread

Preparation Time: 20 minutes
Baking Time: 50 to 60 minutes

- 1 cup sugar
- ½ cup shortening
- 2 eggs
- 1 teaspoon vanilla
- 2 cups all-purpose flour
- 1 teaspoon baking powder
- 1 teaspoon baking soda
- ½ teaspoon salt
- 2 cups chopped peeled apples
- ½ cup chopped nuts
- ⅓ cup dried cherries

Topping

- 1 tablespoon sugar
- ¼ teaspoon ground cinnamon

Preheat oven to 350°F. Grease and flour 9×5×3-inch loaf pan.

Mix 1 cup sugar, shortening, eggs and vanilla in large bowl. Stir in flour, baking powder, baking soda and salt until smooth. Stir in apples, nuts and dried cherries. Spread in prepared pan. Mix 1 tablespoon sugar and cinnamon in small cup or bowl. Sprinkle over batter. Bake until toothpick inserted into center comes out clean (50 to 60 minutes). Immediately remove from pan. Cool completely before slicing. Store tightly covered. *Makes 1 loaf*

Favorite recipe from New York Apple Association, Inc.

Sweet Potato Muffins

  2 cups all-purpose flour
¾ cup chopped walnuts
¾ cup golden raisins
½ cup packed brown sugar
  1 tablespoon baking powder
  1 teaspoon ground cinnamon
½ teaspoon baking soda
½ teaspoon salt
¼ teaspoon ground nutmeg
  1 cup mashed peeled cooked sweet potato
¾ cup milk
½ cup (1 stick) butter, melted
  2 eggs, beaten
1½ teaspoons vanilla

1. Preheat oven to 400°F. Grease 24 standard (2½-inch) muffin cups or line with paper baking cups.

2. Combine flour, walnuts, raisins, brown sugar, baking powder, cinnamon, baking soda, salt and nutmeg in medium bowl; stir until well blended.

3. Combine sweet potato, milk, butter, eggs and vanilla in large bowl; mix well. Add flour mixture; stir just until ingredients are moistened.

4. Spoon batter evenly into prepared muffin cups. Bake 15 minutes or until toothpick inserted into centers comes out clean. Cool in pans on wire racks 5 minutes. Remove to wire racks; cool completely.

Makes 24 muffins

Festive Yule Loaves

2¾ cups all-purpose flour, divided

⅓ cup sugar

1 teaspoon salt

1 package (¼ ounce) active dry yeast

1 cup milk

½ cup (1 stick) butter or margarine

1 egg

½ cup golden raisins

½ cup chopped candied red and green cherries

½ cup chopped pecans

Vanilla Glaze (recipe follows), optional

1. Combine 1½ cups flour, sugar, salt and yeast in large bowl. Heat milk and butter over medium heat until very warm (120° to 130°F). Gradually stir into flour mixture. Add egg. Mix with electric mixer at low speed 1 minute. Beat at high speed 3 minutes, scraping side of bowl frequently. Toss raisins, cherries and pecans with ¼ cup flour in small bowl; stir into batter. Stir in enough of remaining 1 cup flour to make a soft dough. Turn out onto lightly floured surface. Knead about 10 minutes or until smooth and elastic. Place in greased bowl; turn to grease top of dough. Cover with clean kitchen towel. Let rise in warm, draft-free place about 1 hour or until doubled in size.

2. Punch down dough. Divide in half. Roll out each half on lightly floured surface to form 8-inch circle. Fold in half; press only folded edge firmly. Place on ungreased baking sheet. Cover with towel. Let rise in warm, draft-free place about 30 minutes or until doubled in bulk.

3. Preheat oven to 375°F. Bake loaves 20 to 25 minutes or until golden brown. Remove from baking sheet; cool completely on wire racks. Frost with Vanilla Glaze, if desired. Store in airtight containers.

Makes 2 loaves

Vanilla Glaze: Combine 1 cup sifted powdered sugar, 4 to 5 teaspoons light cream or half-and-half and ½ teaspoon vanilla in small bowl; stir until smooth.

Dresden Stollen

¼ cup golden raisins

¼ cup chopped candied cherries

¼ cup slivered almonds

¼ cup candied orange peel

2 tablespoons brandy or rum

¼ cup warm water (105° to 115°F)

4 tablespoons granulated sugar, divided

2 packages (¼ ounce each) active dry yeast

4 pieces pared lemon peel (each about 2×½ inches)

2¾ cups all-purpose flour

⅓ cup cold butter or margarine, cut into 5 pieces

½ teaspoon salt

1 large egg

½ teaspoon almond extract

2 to 5 tablespoons milk

   All-purpose flour

2 tablespoons butter or margarine, melted and divided

1 large egg white, lightly beaten

3 tablespoons powdered sugar

1. Combine raisins, cherries, almonds, orange peel and brandy in small bowl. Set aside.

2. Combine water, 1 tablespoon granulated sugar and yeast. Stir to dissolve yeast. Let stand until bubbly, about 5 minutes.

3. Fit food processor with steel blade. Place remaining 3 tablespoons granulated sugar and lemon peel in work bowl. Process until peel is minced. Add 2¾ cups flour, ⅓ cup butter and salt to sugar mixture in work bowl. Process until mixed, about 15 seconds. Add yeast mixture, egg and almond extract; process until blended, about 10 seconds.

4. Turn on processor. Very slowly drizzle just enough milk through feed tube for dough to form a ball and pull away from side of bowl.

Process until ball turns around bowl about 25 times. Turn off processor. Let dough stand 1 to 2 minutes.

5. Turn on processor. Gradually drizzle in enough remaining milk to make dough soft, smooth and satiny, but not sticky. Process until dough turns around bowl about 15 times.

6. Turn dough out onto lightly floured surface; shape into ball. Cover with inverted bowl or plastic wrap. Let stand 20 minutes.

7. Knead reserved fruit mixture into dough on well-floured surface. Sprinkle with additional flour, if necessary, to keep dough from becoming sticky. Shape dough into ball. Place in lightly greased bowl, turning to grease sides. Cover loosely with plastic wrap. Let stand in warm (85°F), draft-free place until doubled in size, about 1 hour.

8. Punch down dough. Roll or pat dough into 9×7-inch oval on large greased baking sheet. Brush with 1 tablespoon melted butter. Make a crease lengthwise, just off the center, with handle of wooden spoon. Fold lengthwise, bringing smaller section over larger one. Brush top with egg white. Cover loosely with plastic wrap. Let stand in warm, draft-free place until almost doubled, about 45 minutes.

9. Preheat oven to 350°F. Uncover bread; bake 25 to 30 minutes or until evenly browned. Immediately transfer from baking sheet to wire rack. Brush remaining 1 tablespoon melted butter onto bread. Sift powdered sugar over top. Cool.   *Makes 1 loaf*

Stollen is the traditional Christmas bread of Germany.

Delectable Chocolate Wreath

½ cup milk

¼ cup water (70° to 80°F)

3 tablespoons butter or margarine, cut up

1 large egg

⅓ cup sugar

¼ cup unsweetened cocoa powder

¾ teaspoon salt

2½ cups bread flour or all-purpose flour

2 teaspoons FLEISCHMANN'S® Bread Machine Yeast

    White Chocolate, Raspberry and Pecan Filling (recipe follows)

    Frosting (recipe follows)

Bread Machine Directions

Add all ingredients except filling and frosting to bread machine pan in the order suggested by manufacturer. Select dough/manual cycle. When cycle is complete, remove dough to lightly floured surface. If necessary, knead in enough flour to make dough easy to handle.

Roll dough to 22×6-inch rectangle. With sharp knife, cut in half lengthwise to make two 22×3-inch strips. Spread half of White Chocolate, Raspberry and Pecan Filling down center length of each strip. Fold long sides of dough over filling; pinch seams and ends to seal. Place ropes, seam sides down, on greased large baking sheet. Twist ropes together; form into wreath. Pinch ends to seal. Cover and let rise in warm, draft-free place until risen slightly, about 1 hour.

Bake at 350°F for 35 to 40 minutes or until done. Remove from baking sheet; cool on wire rack. Drizzle with frosting.

Makes 1 wreath

White Chocolate, Raspberry and Pecan Filling: Combine ¾ cup white chocolate morsels, ½ cup chopped toasted pecans, and 2 tablespoons seedless red raspberry jam.

Frosting: Combine 1 cup sifted powdered sugar, 1 to 2 tablespoons milk and 1 teaspoon Spice Islands® Pure Vanilla Extract. Stir until smooth.

Dinner Rolls

1½ Pounds Dough

¾ **cup milk**

1 **egg**

⅓ **cup shortening**

1 **teaspoon salt**

3 **cups all-purpose flour**

3 **tablespoons sugar**

1½ **teaspoons active dry yeast**

2 Pounds Dough

1 **cup milk**

2 **eggs**

½ **cup shortening**

1½ **teaspoons salt**

4 **cups all-purpose flour**

¼ **cup sugar**

2 **teaspoons active dry yeast**

Bread Machine Directions

1. Measuring carefully, place all ingredients in bread machine pan in order specified by owner's manual. Program dough cycle setting; press start. For 1½ pounds dough, grease 13×9-inch baking pan; set aside. For 2 pounds dough, grease 2 (8-inch) square baking pans; set aside.

2. When cycle is complete, remove dough to lightly floured surface. If necessary, knead in additional flour to make dough easy to handle. For 1½ pounds dough, divide into 18 equal pieces; for 2 pounds dough, divide into 24 equal pieces. Shape each dough piece into smooth ball. Place in prepared pan(s). Cover with clean kitchen towels; let rise in warm, draft-free place 45 minutes or until doubled in size.

3. Preheat oven to 375°F. Bake rolls 15 to 20 minutes or until golden brown. Remove from pan(s); cool on wire racks.

Makes 18 to 24 rolls

Holiday Treasures

Filling

   1 package (8 ounces) cream cheese, softened

   1 large egg

   ¼ cup sugar

   ½ teaspoon SPICE ISLANDS® Pure Vanilla Extract

   ½ cup dried cranberries or miniature semisweet chocolate pieces

Dough

   2 large eggs

   ¼ cup milk

   3 tablespoons butter or margarine, cut up

   2 tablespoons water

   ¼ teaspoon salt

 2¼ cups all-purpose flour

   4 teaspoons sugar

   2 teaspoons freshly grated orange peel

   ⅛ teaspoon SPICE ISLANDS® Ground Mace

 1½ teaspoons FLEISCHMANN'S® Bread Machine Yeast

Bread Machine Directions

To make filling, combine cream cheese, egg, sugar and vanilla in medium bowl; beat with electric mixer until smooth. Stir in dried cranberries. Cover and refrigerate while preparing dough.

To make dough, add 1 egg, 1 egg yolk (reserve 1 egg white), milk, butter, water, salt, flour, sugar, orange peel, mace and yeast to bread machine pan in the order suggested by manufacturer. Select dough/manual cycle.

To shape, remove dough to lightly floured surface when cycle is complete. If necessary, knead in additional flour to make dough easy to handle. Divide dough into 8 equal pieces; roll each into 6-inch circle. Place 2 rounded tablespoons filling in center of each circle. Bring dough up around filling, pleating and pinching firmly just above filling to seal. Place 2 inches apart on greased baking sheet.

Cover and let rise in warm, draft-free place until doubled in size, about 30 to 40 minutes. Uncover rolls; pinch again, just above filling, to reseal. Lightly beat reserved egg white; brush onto rolls. Bake at 350°F for 20 to 25 minutes or until golden brown. Remove from pan; cool on wire rack.   *Makes 8 sweet rolls*

Cherry Eggnog Quick Bread

2½ cups all-purpose flour

¾ cup sugar

1 tablespoon baking powder

½ teaspoon ground nutmeg

1¼ cups prepared dairy eggnog or half-and-half

6 tablespoons butter, melted and cooled

2 eggs, lightly beaten

1 teaspoon vanilla

½ cup chopped pecans

½ cup coarsely chopped candied red cherries

1. Preheat oven to 350°F. Grease 3 (5½×3-inch) mini-loaf pans.

2. Combine flour, sugar, baking powder and nutmeg in large bowl. Combine eggnog, melted butter, eggs and vanilla in medium bowl; stir until well blended. Add eggnog mixture to flour mixture. Mix just until moistened. Stir in pecans and cherries. Spoon into prepared pans.

3. Bake 35 to 40 minutes or until toothpick inserted into centers comes out clean. Cool in pans 15 minutes. Remove from pans; cool completely on wire racks. Store tightly wrapped in plastic wrap at room temperature.   *Makes 3 mini loaves*

Note: No gift compares to a loaf of homemade bread—especially when it's given in a new loaf pan! Just add a wooden spoon, along with the recipe; then wrap it all up in a festive towel and tie it with colorful holiday ribbon.

Apples and Cheese Rolls

2 cups coarsely chopped Golden Delicious apples

2 tablespoons chopped onion

2 tablespoons margarine

2 teaspoons lemon juice

½ to ¾ teaspoon dried oregano, crushed

½ teaspoon grated lemon peel

¼ teaspoon medium grind pepper

4 ounces (1 cup) shredded mozzarella cheese

1 loaf (14 to 16 ounces) frozen yeast bread dough, thawed

Sauté apples and onion in margarine until apples are barely tender. Add lemon juice, oregano, lemon peel and pepper; mix well. Cool mixture slightly; stir in cheese. Roll dough to 15×8-inch rectangle. Spread apple-cheese mixture over dough, leaving about 1-inch border on 1 (15-inch) side. Starting with opposite 15-inch side, tightly roll up dough jelly-roll fashion; moisten edge with water and seal. Cut into 1½-inch slices. Place slices, cut sides down, on greased baking sheet about 1½ inches apart. Cover and let rise until doubled in size. Bake at 350°F 25 to 30 minutes or until lightly browned. Serve warm.

Makes 15 rolls

Tip: Apples and Cheese Rolls are best served warm. To reheat one roll, loosely wrap in paper towel and microwave on HIGH (100%) 10 to 15 seconds.

*Favorite recipe from **Washington Apple Commission***

Harvest Mini Chip Muffins

¼ cup (½ stick) butter or margarine, softened

1 cup sugar

1 cup canned pumpkin

2 eggs

2¼ cups all-purpose flour

2 teaspoons baking powder

¾ teaspoon pumpkin pie spice

½ teaspoon baking soda

½ teaspoon salt

½ cup milk

1 cup HERSHEY'S MINI CHIPS™ Semi-Sweet Chocolate Chips

½ cup chopped pecans

1. Heat oven to 350°F. Grease or line muffin cups (2½ inches in diameter) with paper bake cups.

2. Beat butter and sugar in large bowl until creamy. Add pumpkin and eggs; blend well. Stir together flour, baking powder, pumpkin pie spice, baking soda and salt; add alternately with milk to pumpkin mixture, beating after each addition just until blended. Stir in mini chocolate chips and pecans. Fill muffin cups ⅔ full with batter.

3. Bake 20 to 25 minutes or until wooden pick inserted into centers comes out clean. Serve warm. *Makes about 2 dozen muffins*

Parker House Rolls

4¾ to 5¼ cups all-purpose flour

⅓ cup sugar

2 envelopes FLEISCHMANN'S® RapidRise™ Yeast

1½ teaspoons salt

¾ cup milk

¾ cup water

¼ cup butter or margarine

1 large egg

¼ cup butter or margarine, melted

In large bowl, combine 2 cups flour, sugar, undissolved yeast and salt. Heat milk, water and ¼ cup unmelted butter until very warm (120° to 130°F). Stir into dry ingredients. Beat 2 minutes at medium speed of electric mixer, scraping bowl occasionally. Add egg and ½ cup flour; beat 2 minutes at high speed. Stir in enough remaining flour to make a soft dough. Knead on lightly floured surface until smooth and elastic, about 8 to 10 minutes. Cover;* let rest 10 minutes.

Divide dough in half; roll each half into 12-inch square, about ¼ inch thick. Cut each into 6 (12×2-inch) strips. Cut each strip into 3 (4×2-inch) rectangles. Brush each rectangle with melted butter. Crease rectangles slightly off center with dull edge of knife and fold at crease. Arrange rolls side by side in rows, slightly overlapping, on greased baking sheets, with shorter side of each roll facing down. Allow ¼ inch of space between each row. Cover; let rise in warm, draft-free place until doubled in size, about 30 minutes.

Bake at 400°F for 13 to 15 minutes or until done. Remove from baking sheets; cool on wire racks. Brush with remaining melted butter.

Makes 36 rolls

*If desired, allow dough to rise in refrigerator 12 to 24 hours.

Libby's® Pumpkin Cranberry Bread

3 cups all-purpose flour

1 tablespoon plus 2 teaspoons pumpkin pie spice

2 teaspoons baking soda

1½ teaspoons salt

3 cups granulated sugar

1 can (15 ounces) LIBBY'S® 100% Pure Pumpkin

4 large eggs

1 cup vegetable oil

½ cup orange juice or water

1 cup sweetened dried, fresh or frozen cranberries

PREHEAT oven to 350°F. Grease and flour two 9×5-inch loaf pans.

COMBINE flour, pumpkin pie spice, baking soda and salt in large bowl. Combine sugar, pumpkin, eggs, vegetable oil and orange juice in large mixer bowl; beat until just blended. Add pumpkin mixture to flour mixture; stir just until moistened. Fold in cranberries. Spoon batter into prepared loaf pans.

BAKE for 60 to 65 minutes or until wooden pick inserted into centers comes out clean. Cool in pans on wire racks for 10 minutes; remove to wire racks to cool completely.   *Makes 2 loaves*

8×4-INCH LOAF PANS: **PREPARE** three 8×4-inch loaf pans as directed above. Bake for 55 to 60 minutes.

5×3-INCH MINI-LOAF PANS: **PREPARE** five or six 5×3-inch mini-loaf pans as directed above. Bake for 50 to 55 minutes.

Cherry Zucchini Bread

  2 eggs

  ¾ cup granulated sugar

  ⅓ cup vegetable oil

  ⅓ cup lemon juice

  ¼ cup water

  2 cups all-purpose flour

  2 teaspoons baking powder

  1 teaspoon ground cinnamon

  ½ teaspoon baking soda

  ¼ teaspoon salt

  ⅔ cup shredded unpeeled zucchini

  ⅔ cup dried tart cherries

  1 tablespoon grated lemon peel

Place eggs in large mixing bowl. Beat with electric mixer on medium speed 3 to 4 minutes or until eggs are thick and lemon colored. Add sugar, oil, lemon juice and water; mix well. Combine flour, baking powder, cinnamon, baking soda and salt. Add flour mixture to egg mixture; mix well. Stir in zucchini, cherries and lemon peel.

Grease and flour bottom of 8½×4½-inch loaf pan. Pour batter into prepared pan. Bake in preheated 350°F oven 55 to 65 minutes or until wooden toothpick inserted into center comes out clean. Let cool in pan on wire rack 10 minutes. Loosen edges with metal spatula. Remove from pan. Let cool completely. Wrap tightly in plastic wrap and store in refrigerator.   *Makes 1 loaf (about 16 servings)*

Favorite recipe from **Cherry Marketing Institute**

Harvest Stuffing Bread

3 cups all-purpose flour

1 envelope FLEISCHMANN'S® RapidRise™ Yeast

2 tablespoons plus 1 teaspoon instant minced onions, divided

1 tablespoon sugar

1 tablespoon parsley flakes

1½ teaspoons poultry seasoning

1 teaspoon salt

1¼ cups water

1 tablespoon butter or margarine

1 egg, beaten

½ teaspoon whole celery seed

In large bowl, combine 2 cups flour, undissolved yeast, 2 tablespoons onions, sugar, parsley flakes, poultry seasoning and salt. Heat water and butter until very warm (120° to 130°F). Stir into dry ingredients. Beat 2 minutes at medium speed of electric mixer, scraping bowl occasionally. Stir in remaining flour to make stiff batter. Cover; let rest 10 minutes.

Turn batter into greased 1½-quart casserole. Smooth top of dough in casserole with floured hands. Cover; let rise in warm, draft-free place until doubled in size, about 30 minutes. Brush beaten egg on loaf. Sprinkle with remaining onions and celery seed. Bake at 375°F* for 35 minutes or until done. Remove from casserole; cool on wire rack.

Makes 1 loaf

Bake at 350°F if glass casserole is used.

Whole Wheat Herbed Bread Wreath

1½-Pound Loaf

- 1 cup water
- 1 tablespoon olive oil
- 1 teaspoon salt
- 2¼ cups all-purpose flour
- ¾ cup whole wheat flour
- 1 tablespoon sugar
- 2 teaspoons crushed dried rosemary
- 1½ teaspoons active dry yeast

2-Pound Loaf

- 1¼ cups water
- 2 tablespoons olive oil
- 1½ teaspoons salt
- 3 cups all-purpose flour
- 1 cup whole wheat flour
- 2 tablespoons sugar
- 3 teaspoons crushed dried rosemary
- 2 teaspoons active dry yeast

Glaze

- 1 egg, beaten
- 1 tablespoon water

Bread Machine Directions

1. Measuring carefully, place all ingredients (except glaze ingredients) for desired loaf size in bread machine pan in order specified by owner's manual. Program dough cycle setting; press start. Grease large baking sheet and 10-ounce ovenproof round bowl; set aside.

2. When cycle is complete, remove dough to lightly floured surface. If necessary, knead in additional all-purpose flour to make dough easy to handle. Divide dough into thirds. Roll each piece to form 24-inch rope. Place on prepared baking sheet. Braid ropes, beginning at center

and working toward ends. Seal edges. Shape into circle around prepared ovenproof bowl. Seal ends well. Cover with clean kitchen towel; let rise in warm, draft-free place 45 minutes or until doubled in size.

3. Preheat oven to 375°F.

4. Meanwhile, for glaze, combine egg and water in small bowl; brush over wreath. Bake 25 to 35 minutes or until golden brown. Cool on baking sheet 10 minutes. Remove from baking sheet and bowl; cool on wire rack.

Makes 1 loaf

Apricot Holiday Bread

⅔ **cup milk**

1 **egg**

2 **tablespoons butter, softened**

1 **teaspoon salt**

3 **cups all-purpose flour**

½ **cup pecan or walnut pieces**

½ **cup dried apricots or peaches, chopped**

2 **tablespoons sugar**

¼ **teaspoon ground ginger**

¼ **teaspoon ground nutmeg**

1 **tablespoon active dry yeast**

Bread Machine Directions

1. Measuring carefully, place all ingredients in bread machine pan in order specified by owner's manual.

2. Program basic or white cycle and desired crust setting; press start. (Do not use delay cycle.)

3. Remove baked bread from pan; cool on wire rack.

Makes 1 (1½-pound) loaf (12 to 16 servings)

Cheery Cranberry Chocolate Chip Bread

1 cup HERSHEY'S Semi-Sweet Chocolate Chips

1 cup fresh or frozen cranberries, coarsely chopped

½ cup pecan pieces

2 teaspoons freshly grated orange peel

2 cups all-purpose flour

1 cup sugar

1½ teaspoons baking powder

½ teaspoon baking soda

½ teaspoon salt

2 tablespoons shortening

¾ cup orange juice

1 egg, slightly beaten

Cocoa Drizzle Glaze (recipe follows)

1. Heat oven to 350°F. Grease and flour three 5¾×3¼×2-inch miniature loaf pans.

2. Stir together chocolate chips, cranberries, pecans and orange peel in small bowl; set aside.

3. Stir together flour, sugar, baking powder, baking soda and salt in large bowl; with pastry blender, cut in shortening until mixture resembles coarse crumbs. Stir in orange juice, egg and reserved chocolate chip mixture just until moistened; divide evenly among prepared pans.

4. Bake 40 to 45 minutes or until wooden pick inserted into centers comes out clean. Cool 15 minutes; remove from pans to wire rack. Cool completely. Drizzle Cocoa Drizzle Glaze over top.

Makes 3 loaves

Cocoa Drizzle Glaze

1 tablespoon butter or margarine

1 tablespoon HERSHEY'S Cocoa or HERSHEY'S SPECIAL DARK® Cocoa

1 tablespoon water

½ cup powdered sugar

½ teaspoon vanilla extract

1. Microwave butter in small microwave-safe bowl at HIGH (100%) 20 to 30 seconds until melted. Stir in cocoa and water. Microwave at HIGH 15 to 30 seconds or just until mixture is hot, slightly thickened and smooth when stirred. Do not boil.

2. Gradually add powdered sugar and vanilla, beating with whisk until smooth. If necessary, add water, a few drops at a time, until of desired consistency.   *Makes about ¼ cup glaze*

Use the on/off pulsing action of a food processor fitted with a chopping blade to quickly and easily chop the cranberries for this scrumptious recipe.

Spicy Mincemeat Bread

6 tablespoons butter, softened

1 cup packed light brown sugar

2 eggs

1 teaspoon vanilla

2½ cups all-purpose flour

1½ teaspoons baking soda

1 teaspoon ground cinnamon

¾ teaspoon baking powder

½ teaspoon ground nutmeg

¼ teaspoon salt

¾ cup sour cream

1 cup prepared mincemeat

¾ cup chopped pecans

1. Preheat oven to 350°F. Grease 9×5-inch loaf pan.*

2. Beat butter and brown sugar in large bowl with electric mixer at medium speed until light and fluffy. Beat in eggs and vanilla until blended.

3. Combine flour, baking soda, cinnamon, baking powder, nutmeg and salt in medium bowl. With mixer on low speed, add flour mixture to butter mixture alternately with sour cream, beginning and ending with flour mixture. Mix well after each addition.

4. Mix in mincemeat and pecans on low speed until blended. Spoon into prepared pan.

5. Bake 55 to 60 minutes or until toothpick inserted into center comes out clean. Cool in pan 15 minutes. Remove from pan to wire rack; cool completely. Store tightly wrapped in plastic wrap at room temperature.   *Makes 1 loaf*

Bread may also be baked in 4 (5½×3-inch) greased mini-loaf pans. Prepare batter as directed. Bake at 350°F for 45 to 50 minutes or until toothpick inserted into centers comes out clean. Cool as directed.

Holiday Rye Bread

3 to 3½ cups all-purpose flour

2½ cups rye flour

⅓ cup sugar

2 envelopes FLEISCHMANN'S® RapidRise™ Yeast

1 tablespoon grated orange peel

2½ teaspoons salt

2 teaspoons fennel seed

1 cup beer or malt liquor

½ cup water

¼ cup light molasses

2 tablespoons butter or margarine

Molasses Glaze (recipe follows)

In large bowl, combine 1½ cups all-purpose flour, rye flour, sugar, undissolved yeast, orange peel, salt and fennel seed. Heat beer, water, molasses and butter until very warm (120° to 130°F). Stir into dry ingredients. Beat 2 minutes at medium speed of electric mixer, scraping bowl occasionally. Stir in enough remaining flour to make soft dough. Knead on lightly floured surface until smooth and elastic, about 8 to 10 minutes. Cover; let rest 10 minutes.

Divide dough into 4 equal pieces. Roll each to 10×6-inch oval. Roll each up tightly from long side, as for jelly roll, tapering ends. Pinch seams to seal. Place on greased baking sheets. Cover; let rise in warm, draft-free place until doubled in size, about 1½ hours.

With sharp knife, make 3 diagonal cuts on top of each loaf. Brush with Molasses Glaze. Bake at 375°F for 15 minutes; brush loaves with Glaze. Bake additional 10 minutes or until done. Remove loaves from oven and brush again with Glaze. Cool on wire racks.

Makes 4 small loaves

Molasses Glaze: Combine 2 tablespoons molasses and 2 tablespoons water. Stir until well blended.

Fruitcake Cookies

¾ **cup sugar**

½ **cup (1 stick) butter, softened**

½ **cup milk**

1 **egg**

2 **tablespoons orange juice**

1 **tablespoon cider vinegar**

2 **cups all-purpose flour**

1 **teaspoon baking powder**

½ **teaspoon baking soda**

¼ **teaspoon salt**

½ **cup chopped walnuts**

½ **cup** *each* **raisins and chopped candied mixed fruit**

¼ **cup chopped dried pineapple**

Powdered sugar

1. Preheat oven to 350°F. Grease cookie sheets. Beat sugar and butter in large bowl until creamy. Beat in milk, egg, orange juice and vinegar until blended. Mix in flour, baking powder, baking soda and salt. Stir in walnuts, raisins, mixed fruit and pineapple.

2. Drop rounded tablespoonfuls of dough 2 inches apart onto cookie sheets. Bake 12 to 14 minutes or until lightly browned around edges. Cool 2 minutes on cookie sheets. Remove to wire racks; cool completely. Dust with powdered sugar. Store in airtight container. *Makes about 2½ dozen cookies*

Fruitcake Cookies

Browned Butter Spritz Cookies

1½ cups (3 sticks) butter
½ cup granulated sugar
¼ cup powdered sugar
1 egg yolk
1 teaspoon vanilla
⅛ teaspoon almond extract
2½ cups all-purpose flour
¼ cup cake flour
¼ teaspoon salt

1. Heat butter in medium heavy saucepan over medium heat until melted and light amber in color, stirring frequently. Transfer butter to large bowl. Cover and refrigerate about 2 hours or until solid. Let butter stand at room temperature about 15 minutes to soften before completing recipe.

2. Preheat oven to 350°F. Beat browned butter, granulated sugar and powdered sugar in large bowl with electric mixer at medium speed until light and fluffy. Add egg yolk, vanilla and almond extract; beat until well blended.

3. Combine all-purpose flour, cake flour and salt in small bowl. Add flour mixture to butter mixture; beat until well blended.

4. Fit cookie press with desired plate (or change plates for different shapes after first batch). Fill press with dough; press dough spritz 1 inch apart onto ungreased cookie sheets. Bake 10 to 12 minutes or until just lightly browned. Cool 5 minutes on cookie sheets. Remove to wire racks; cool completely.   *Makes about 8 dozen cookies*

Decorating Tip: Add holiday sparkle to these delicious cookies. Sprinkle them with red or green decorating sugar or press red or green glacé cherry halves into centers before baking. For pretty trees or wreaths, tint the dough with green food coloring before using the tree or wreath plate in your cookie press. Sprinkle with colored nonpareils (for ornaments) before baking, or pipe red icing bows on the baked and cooled cookies.

Premier Cheesecake Cranberry Bars

2 cups all-purpose flour

1½ cups quick or old-fashioned oats

¼ cup packed light brown sugar

1 cup (2 sticks) butter or margarine, softened

2 cups (12-ounce package) NESTLÉ® TOLL HOUSE® Premier White Morsels

1 package (8 ounces) cream cheese, softened

1 can (14 ounces) NESTLÉ® CARNATION® Sweetened Condensed Milk

¼ cup lemon juice

1 teaspoon vanilla extract

1 can (16 ounces) whole-berry cranberry sauce

2 tablespoons cornstarch

PREHEAT oven to 350°F. Grease 13×9-inch baking pan.

COMBINE flour, oats and brown sugar in large bowl. Add butter; mix until crumbly. Stir in morsels. Reserve *2½ cups* morsel mixture for topping. With floured fingers, press *remaining* mixture into prepared pan.

BEAT cream cheese in large mixer bowl until creamy. Add sweetened condensed milk, lemon juice and vanilla extract; mix until smooth. Pour over crust. Combine cranberry sauce and cornstarch in medium bowl. Spoon over cream cheese mixture. Sprinkle *reserved* morsel mixture over cranberry mixture.

BAKE for 35 to 40 minutes or until center is set. Cool completely in pan on wire rack. Cover; refrigerate until serving time (up to 1 day). Cut into bars. *Makes 2½ dozen bars*

Soft Ginger Cookies

    2 cups flour

1½ teaspoons ground ginger

    1 teaspoon baking soda

  ¼ teaspoon salt

  ¼ teaspoon ground cinnamon

  ¼ teaspoon ground cloves

  ¼ cup packed brown sugar

  ¼ cup canola oil

  ¼ cup molasses

    1 egg white

  ½ cup fat-free sour cream

     Nonstick cooking spray

1. Preheat oven to 350°F.

2. Combine flour, ginger, baking soda, salt, cinnamon and cloves in large bowl; set aside.

3. Beat brown sugar, oil and molasses together in large bowl with electric mixer at medium speed until smooth. Beat in egg white and sour cream until well blended.

4. Slowly add flour mixture to oil mixture, beating at low speed until well blended and scraping down side of bowl occasionally.

5. Drop dough by level tablespoonfuls onto ungreased baking sheets. Flatten dough to ⅛-inch thickness with bottom of small glass lightly sprayed with cooking spray.

6. Bake 10 minutes or until tops of cookies have puffed up and spring back when lightly touched. Let cool on baking sheets 2 minutes. Transfer to wire racks; cool completely.

Makes about 3 dozen cookies

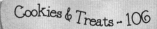

Almond-Orange Shortbread

1 **cup (4 ounces) sliced almonds, divided**

2 **cups all-purpose flour**

1 **cup (2 sticks) cold butter, cut into pieces**

½ **cup sugar**

½ **cup cornstarch**

2 **tablespoons grated orange peel**

1 **teaspoon almond extract**

1. Preheat oven to 350°F.

2. Spread ¾ cup almonds in single layer in large baking pan. Bake 6 minutes or until golden brown, stirring frequently. Remove pan from oven to wire rack. Cool completely in pan. *Reduce oven temperature to 325°F.*

3. Place toasted almonds in food processor. Process, using on/off pulses, until almonds are coarsely chopped. Add flour, butter, sugar, cornstarch, orange peel and almond extract to food processor. Process, using on/off pulses, until mixture resembles coarse crumbs.

4. Press dough firmly and evenly into 10×8¾-inch rectangle on large ungreased cookie sheet. Score dough into 1¼-inch squares. Press one slice of remaining almonds in center of each square.

5. Bake 30 to 40 minutes or until shortbread is firm when pressed and lightly browned. Immediately cut into squares along score lines with sharp knife. Remove cookies to wire racks; cool completely. Store loosely covered at room temperature up to 1 week.

Makes about 4½ dozen cookies

Sugared Pecan Halves

1½ **cups sugar**

½ **cup orange juice**

2 **tablespoons CRISCO® Butter Flavor Shortening**

2 **tablespoons light corn syrup**

½ **teaspoon ground cinnamon**

¼ **teaspoon ground cloves**

2 **packages (6 ounces each) pecan halves (4 cups)**

In 2-quart saucepan combine sugar, orange juice, CRISCO Shortening, corn syrup, cinnamon and cloves. Cook over medium heat, stirring constantly, to 240°F on candy thermometer. Stir in pecans. Pour onto greased baking sheet, spreading to thin layer. Cool completely. Break to separate nuts. *Makes 4 cups*

Always read a candy thermometer at eye level, where you're sure to get the most accurate reading.

Candy Cane Biscotti

1 cup sugar

½ cup (1 stick) butter, softened

2 eggs

2 tablespoons water

1 teaspoon peppermint extract

3½ cups all-purpose flour

1 cup finely crushed peppermint candy canes, divided

½ cup slivered almonds, toasted*

1 teaspoon baking powder

½ teaspoon salt

4 squares (1 ounce each) white chocolate, melted

*To toast nuts, spread in single layer on baking sheet and toast in preheated 350°F oven 8 to 10 minutes or until very lightly browned. Or, place nuts in microwavable dish. Heat on HIGH 1 to 2 minutes or just until light golden brown, stirring nuts every 30 seconds. Allow to stand 3 minutes. The nuts will darken and become more crisp as they cool.

1. Preheat oven to 350°F. Line 2 cookie sheets with parchment paper.

2. Combine sugar, butter, eggs, water and peppermint extract in large bowl. Beat with electric mixer at medium speed until well blended. Add flour, ½ cup crushed candy canes, almonds, baking powder and salt. Beat at low speed until just blended.

3. Divide dough in half. Shape each half into 10×3-inch log. Place 1 log on each cookie sheet. Bake 30 minutes or until centers are firm to the touch. Let cool 15 to 20 minutes.

4. Using serrated knife, cut logs diagonally into ½-inch-thick slices. Place slices, cut sides down, on prepared cookie sheets. Bake 15 minutes. Turn and bake 12 to 15 minutes longer or until edges are browned. Cool completely on wire racks.

5. Dip each cookie halfway in melted chocolate. Sprinkle each cookie with remaining ½ cup crushed candy canes. Store in tightly covered container.   *Makes 40 cookies*

Cherry Cheesecake Swirl Bars

Crust

1⅔ cups graham cracker crumbs (about 25 [2½-inch] square
    graham crackers, crushed)

6 tablespoons butter, melted

3 tablespoons sugar

Cheesecake

2 packages (8 ounces each) cream cheese, softened

½ cup sugar

2 eggs

1 egg yolk

⅓ cup sour cream

1 tablespoon all-purpose flour

½ teaspoon almond extract

3 tablespoons strained cherry preserves, melted

1. Preheat oven to 325°F. Combine graham cracker crumbs, butter
and 3 tablespoons sugar in 9-inch square baking pan until crumbly.
Press onto pan bottom. Bake 8 minutes or until set but not brown.
Remove from oven; cool.

2. Beat cream cheese in medium bowl with electric mixer at medium
speed. Add ½ cup sugar; beat until smooth, scraping down side of
bowl as needed. Add eggs, yolk, sour cream, flour and almond extract;
beat until well blended, scraping down side of bowl as needed. Spread
cream cheese batter over cooled crust.

3. Drizzle melted preserves in zigzag pattern over cream cheese batter.
Drag knife tip through batter and jam to make swirled pattern.

4. Bake in water bath 45 minutes or until knife inserted 1 inch from
edge comes out clean.   *Makes 16 servings*

Variation: Substitute any seedless jam for the cherry preserves, and
use vanilla extract instead of almond extract.

White Coated Chocolate Truffles

Prep Time: 1 hour
Cook Time: 3 minutes
Cool Time: 10 minutes
Chill Time: 5 hours

- ½ **cup whipping cream**
- 3 **tablespoons butter**
- 1 **cup HERSHEY'S Semi-Sweet Chocolate Chips**
- 1 **teaspoon vanilla extract**
- **White Coating (recipe follows)**

1. Combine whipping cream and butter in medium saucepan. Cook over medium heat, stirring constantly, just until mixture begins to boil; remove from heat. Add chocolate chips, stirring until completely melted; continue stirring until mixture cools and thickens slightly. Stir in vanilla. Pour into shallow glass dish. Cover; refrigerate until firm.

2. To form truffles, with spoon, scoop mixture; shape into 1-inch balls. Place on wax paper-lined tray. Cover; refrigerate until firm. Prepare White Coating. Dip truffles into coating; refrigerate. Serve well chilled. Store in tightly covered container in refrigerator.

Makes about 2 dozen truffles

White Coating: Combine 2 cups (12-ounce package) HERSHEY'S Premier White Chips with 1 tablespoon shortening (do not use butter, margarine, spread or oil) in small microwave-safe bowl. Microwave at HIGH (100%) 1 minute or just until chips are melted when stirred. (Coating works best for dipping between 85° and 90°F. If coating goes below 85°F, place bowl in larger bowl containing warm water; stir coating until temperature reaches 85°F. Be careful not to get any water into coating mixture.)

Peppermint Taffy

  2 tablespoons butter, softened, divided

  ½ cup powdered sugar

2½ cups granulated sugar

  ½ cup water

  ¼ cup distilled white vinegar

  7 to 8 drops red food coloring

  ½ teaspoon peppermint extract

1. Grease 12-inch ceramic oval platter or dish with 1 tablespoon butter. Line large baking sheet with foil; sprinkle evenly with powdered sugar.

2. Combine granulated sugar, water, vinegar and remaining 1 tablespoon butter in heavy 2- or 2½-quart saucepan. Bring to a boil, stirring frequently. Attach candy thermometer to side of pan, making sure bulb is submerged in sugar mixture, but not touching bottom of pan. Continue boiling, without stirring, about 10 minutes or until sugar mixture reaches between hard-ball stage (265°F) and soft-crack stage (270°F) on candy thermometer. Remove from heat; stir in food coloring and peppermint extract.

3. Slowly pour hot sugar mixture onto prepared platter. Let stand 20 to 25 minutes or until cool enough to handle and an indent made with your finger holds its shape.

4. Remove all jewelry as candy will stick to it. With liberally buttered hands, carefully pick up taffy and shape into a ball. (Center of candy may still be very warm but will cool quickly upon handling.) Scrape up any taffy that sticks to plate with rubber spatula.

5. Begin to pull taffy into thick rope about 18 inches long while turning and twisting taffy back on itself. Continue pulling about 10 to 15 minutes or until taffy lightens in color, has satiny finish and is stiff. (It is important to be patient and pull taffy long enough or it will be sticky.)

6. When taffy begins to hold the folds of the rope shape and develops ridges in the rope, begin pulling 1-inch-wide ropes from taffy and let ropes fall onto prepared powdered sugar surface. Using buttered

kitchen shears, cut taffy ropes into 1-inch pieces. Cool completely; wrap pieces individually in waxed paper. Store in airtight container at room temperature up to 1 week.   *Makes about 1 pound taffy*

Lemon Taffy: Substitute 4 to 5 drops yellow food coloring for red food coloring and lemon extract for peppermint extract. Proceed as directed.

Toffee Popcorn Crunch

    8 **cups popped popcorn**
    ¾ **cup whole or slivered almonds**
    1⅓ **cups (8-ounce package) HEATH® BITS 'O BRICKLE® Almond Toffee Bits**
    ½ **cup light corn syrup**

1. Heat oven to 275°F. Grease large roasting pan or two 13×9×2-inch baking pans. Place popcorn and almonds in prepared pan.

2. Combine toffee bits and corn syrup in heavy medium saucepan. Cook over medium heat, stirring constantly, until toffee melts (about 12 minutes). Pour over popcorn mixture; stir until evenly coated.

3. Bake 30 minutes, stirring frequently. Remove from oven; stir every 2 minutes until slightly cooled. Cool completely. Store in tightly covered container in cool, dry place.

Makes about 1 pound popcorn

Note: For best results, do not double this recipe.

Chocolate Gingerbread Cookies

½ cup (1 stick) butter, softened

½ cup packed light brown sugar

¼ cup granulated sugar

1 tablespoon shortening

4 ounces semisweet chocolate, melted and cooled

1 egg

2 tablespoons molasses

2¼ cups all-purpose flour

3 tablespoons unsweetened cocoa powder

2½ teaspoons ground ginger

½ teaspoon baking soda

½ teaspoon ground cinnamon

⅛ teaspoon *each* salt and black pepper

Prepared icing (optional)

1. Beat butter, sugars and shortening in large bowl with electric mixer at medium speed until creamy. Add chocolate; beat until blended. Add egg and molasses; beat until well blended. Combine flour, cocoa, ginger, baking soda, cinnamon, salt and pepper in medium bowl. Gradually add flour mixture to butter mixture, beating until well blended. Divide dough in half. Wrap each half in plastic wrap; refrigerate at least 1 hour.

2. Preheat oven to 350°F. Roll out half of dough between sheets of plastic wrap to about ¼-inch thickness. Cut out shapes with 5-inch cookie cutters. Place cutouts on ungreased cookie sheets. Refrigerate at least 15 minutes. Repeat with remaining dough.

3. Bake 8 to 10 minutes or until cookies are slightly puffed and have small crackles on surfaces. Cool 5 minutes on cookie sheets; remove to wire racks to cool completely. Decorate cooled cookies with icing, if desired. *Makes about 2 dozen cookies*

Chewy Chocolate Gingerbread Drops: Decrease flour to 1¾ cups. Shape 1½ teaspoonfuls of dough into balls. Place on ungreased cookie sheets. Flatten balls slightly, and do not refrigerate before baking. Bake as directed above. *Makes about 4½ dozen cookies*

Classic Coconut Bonbons

2 packages (1 pound each) powdered sugar (about 8 cups), divided

1 can (14 ounces) sweetened condensed milk

½ cup (1 stick) butter

2 teaspoons vanilla

2 cups flaked coconut

1 cup finely chopped pecans or walnuts

2 pounds premium bittersweet chocolate

1. Sift half of powdered sugar into large bowl with fine-meshed sieve or sifter; set aside.

2. Place sweetened condensed milk and butter in small saucepan; cook over low heat until butter melts and mixture is blended, stirring frequently. Remove from heat; stir in vanilla.

3. Pour hot butter mixture over reserved powdered sugar; beat with electric mixer at medium speed until blended. Sift remaining powdered sugar into bowl; continue to beat until blended and creamy. Stir in coconut and pecans with wooden spoon until combined. Cover with plastic wrap; refrigerate 1 hour.

4. Shape coconut mixture into 1-inch balls. Place on baking sheet lined with waxed paper. Refrigerate until firm.

5. Temper chocolate.

6. Dip balls in tempered chocolate with dipping fork or spoon, tapping handle against side of pan to allow excess chocolate to drain back into pan.

7. Remove excess chocolate by scraping bottom of bonbon across rim of saucepan.

8. Place bonbons on waxed paper; sign bonbons, if desired. Let stand in cool place until chocolate is firm. (Do not refrigerate.) Store in airtight container at room temperature.

Makes about 10 dozen bonbons (4½ pounds)

Fancy Cherry-Pecan Cookies

1 cup packed brown sugar

¾ cup shortening

1 egg

1 teaspoon vanilla

½ cup chopped pecans

¼ cup chopped maraschino cherries

2 cups sifted all-purpose flour

½ teaspoon baking soda

½ teaspoon cream of tartar

½ teaspoon salt

1. Beat brown sugar, shortening, egg and vanilla in large bowl with electric mixer at medium speed until fluffy. Stir in pecans and cherries.

2. Sift together flour, baking soda, cream of tartar and salt in medium bowl; add by ½ cupfuls to shortening mixture, beating well after each addition.

3. Divide dough in half. Place each half on sheet of waxed paper; shape into logs. Refrigerate until firm.

4. Preheat oven to 400°F. Cut dough into ⅛-inch-thick slices. Place on *ungreased* cookie sheets. Bake 6 to 8 minutes or until light golden brown. Cool 1 to 2 minutes on cookie sheets. Remove to wire racks; cool completely.   *Makes about 5 dozen cookies*

Holiday Walnut Berry Bites

Prep Time: 30 minutes
Bake Time: 30 minutes

      MAZOLA® No Stick Cooking Spray
2½ cups all-purpose flour
  1 cup cold margarine, cut into pieces
  ½ cup confectioners' sugar
  ½ teaspoon salt
1⅓ cups KARO® Light Corn Syrup
  1 cup granulated sugar
  4 eggs
  3 tablespoons butter, melted
  2 cups fresh or thawed frozen cranberries, coarsely chopped
  1 cup walnuts, chopped
  1 cup white chocolate chips

Preheat oven to 350°F. Spray 15×10×1-inch baking pan with cooking spray. In a large bowl, beat flour, margarine, confectioners' sugar and salt at medium speed until mixture resembles coarse crumbs; press firmly and evenly into pan. Bake 20 minutes or until golden brown.

In a large bowl, beat Karo, granulated sugar, eggs and butter until well blended. Stir in cranberries and walnuts.

Spread mixture evenly over hot crust. Sprinkle with white chocolate chips. Bake 25 to 30 minutes or until set. Cool completely on a wire rack before serving.   *Makes 4 dozen bar cookies*

Pumpkin Cheesecake Squares

1½ cups gingersnap crumbs, plus extra for garnish

6 tablespoons butter, melted

¼ cup plus 2 tablespoons sugar, divided

2 eggs

2½ teaspoons vanilla, divided

1 package (8 ounces) plus 1 package (3 ounces) cream cheese, softened and divided

1¼ cups solid-pack pumpkin

1 teaspoon ground cinnamon

¼ teaspoon ground ginger

¼ teaspoon ground nutmeg

¼ teaspoon ground cloves

1 cup sour cream

1. Preheat oven to 325°F. Lightly grease 13×9-inch baking pan.

2. Combine gingersnap crumbs and butter in small bowl until crumbly. Press into bottom of prepared baking pan. Bake 10 minutes.

3. Meanwhile, place ¼ cup sugar, eggs and 1½ teaspoons vanilla in food processor or blender; process about 1 minute or until smooth. Add cream cheese and pumpkin; process until thoroughly blended. Stir in spices. Pour mixture evenly over hot crust. Bake 40 minutes.

4. Meanwhile, for topping, whisk sour cream, remaining 2 tablespoons sugar and 1 teaspoon vanilla in small bowl until blended. Remove pan from oven; spread sour cream mixture evenly over cheesecake surface. Bake 5 minutes. Turn off oven; open door halfway and let pan cool in oven. When cool, refrigerate 2 hours. Sprinkle with extra gingersnap crumbs; cut into 1-inch squares.   *Makes 35 (1-inch) squares*

Candy Cane Fudge

½ cup whipping cream

½ cup light corn syrup

3 cups (18 ounces) semisweet chocolate chips

1½ cups powdered sugar, sifted

1 cup crushed peppermint candy canes

1½ teaspoons vanilla

1. Line 8-inch baking pan with foil, extending edges over sides of pan.

2. Bring cream and corn syrup to a boil in 2-quart saucepan over medium heat; boil 1 minute. Remove from heat. Stir in chocolate. Cook until chocolate is melted, stirring constantly.

3. Stir in powdered sugar, candy canes and vanilla. Pour into prepared pan. Spread mixture into corners. Cover; refrigerate 2 hours or until firm.

4. Lift fudge out of pan using foil; remove foil. Cut into 1-inch squares. Store in airtight container.   *Makes about 2 pounds (64 pieces)*

Care should be taken when boiling syrup because the hot syrup can cause serious burns if spilled or spattered.

Cherry Walnut
White Chocolate Fudge

3 cups sugar

1 cup whipping cream

½ cup (1 stick) butter

¼ cup light corn syrup

8 ounces premium white chocolate, chopped

1 teaspoon vanilla

1 cup chopped dried cherries

1 cup toasted walnuts, chopped

1. Spray 9-inch square baking pan with nonstick cooking spray. Spray inside of large heavy saucepan.

2. Combine sugar, cream, butter and syrup in prepared saucepan. Cook over medium heat until sugar dissolves and mixture comes to a boil, stirring frequently. Wash down sugar crystals.

3. Attach candy thermometer to side of pan, making sure bulb is submerged in sugar mixture but not touching bottom of pan.

4. Continue cooking about 6 minutes or until sugar mixture reaches soft-ball stage (234°F) on candy thermometer, stirring frequently.

5. Remove from heat; let stand 10 minutes. (Do not stir.)

6. Add white chocolate and vanilla; stir 1 minute or until chocolate is melted and mixture is smooth. Stir in cherries and walnuts.

7. Spread mixture evenly in prepared pan. Score into 64 squares while fudge is still warm. Refrigerate until firm. Cut along score lines into squares.   *Makes 64 pieces*

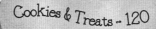

Creamy Caramels

½ cup slivered or chopped toasted almonds (optional)

1 cup (2 sticks) butter or margarine, cut into small pieces

1 can (14 ounces) sweetened condensed milk

2 cups sugar

1 cup light corn syrup

1½ teaspoons vanilla

1. Line 8-inch square baking pan with foil, extending edges over sides of pan. Lightly grease foil; sprinkle almonds over bottom of pan, if desired.

2. Melt butter in heavy 2-quart saucepan over low heat. Add sweetened condensed milk, sugar and corn syrup. Stir over low heat until sugar is dissolved and mixture comes to a boil.

3. Attach candy thermometer to side of pan, making sure bulb is submerged in sugar mixture but not touching bottom of pan. Cook over low heat about 30 minutes or until thermometer registers 240°F (soft-ball stage), stirring occasionally. Immediately remove from heat and stir in vanilla. Pour mixture into prepared pan. Cool completely.

4. Using foil, lift caramels out of pan; remove foil. Place caramels on cutting board; cut into 1-inch squares. Wrap each square in plastic wrap. Store in airtight container.

Makes about 2½ pounds (64 caramels)

Marbled Caramels: Before cooling, top with ⅓ cup chocolate chips; let soften. Use knife to lightly swirl chocolate into caramel. Do not overswirl.

Pinwheel Cookies

- **1 cup (2 sticks) butter, softened**
- **1 package (8 ounces) cream cheese, softened**
- **2 cups all-purpose flour**
- **¼ teaspoon salt**
- **½ cup sugar, divided**
- **½ cup seedless raspberry jam**

1. Beat butter in large bowl until smooth. Add cream cheese; beat until combined and smooth, scraping down side of bowl occasionally.

2. Combine flour and salt in small bowl. Slowly add to butter mixture, beating until combined.

3. Divide dough in half; shape each half into rectangle. Wrap each rectangle in plastic wrap. Chill at least 30 minutes.

4. Preheat oven to 350°F. Grease 2 cookie sheets.

5. Sprinkle ¼ cup sugar on work surface. Roll out 1 dough rectangle on sugared surface to 16-inch square. Trim edges; cut into 25 squares. Form cookie by folding and pressing each corner to middle of square. Transfer to prepared cookie sheets. Repeat with remaining sugar and dough.

6. Bake 20 to 30 minutes. Remove from oven. Place about ½ teaspoon jam in each cookie center. Return to oven; bake 5 to 10 minutes or until golden brown. Remove to wire racks; cool completely.

Makes 50 cookies

Variation: Use cinnamon, sugar and nuts in place of the jam. Sprinkle them over the squares in place of the jam *before* forming the pinwheels. Make sure the nuts are finely chopped.

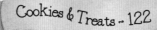

Chocolate Cherry Bars

1 cup (2 sticks) butter or margarine

¾ cup HERSHEY'S Cocoa or HERSHEY'S Special Dark® Cocoa

2 cups sugar

4 eggs

1½ cups plus ⅓ cup all-purpose flour, divided

⅓ cup chopped almonds

1 can (14 ounces) sweetened condensed milk (not evaporated milk)

½ teaspoon almond extract

1 cup HERSHEY'S MINI KISSES® Brand Milk Chocolates

1 cup chopped maraschino cherries, drained

1. Heat oven to 350°F. Generously grease 13×9×2-inch baking pan.

2. Melt butter in large saucepan over low heat; stir in cocoa until smooth. Remove from heat. Add sugar, 3 eggs, 1½ cups flour and almonds; mix well. Pour into prepared pan. Bake 20 minutes.

3. Meanwhile, whisk together remaining 1 egg, remaining ⅓ cup flour, sweetened condensed milk and almond extract. Pour over baked layer; sprinkle chocolate pieces and cherries over top. Return to oven.

4. Bake additional 20 to 25 minutes or until set and edges are golden brown. Cool completely in pan on wire rack. Refrigerate until cold, 6 hours or overnight. Cut into bars. Cover; refrigerate leftover bars.

Makes about 48 bars

Eggnog Fudge

¾ **cup prepared eggnog**

2 **tablespoons light corn syrup**

2 **tablespoons butter or margarine**

2 **cups sugar**

1 **teaspoon vanilla**

1. Butter 8-inch square baking pan. Lightly butter inside of medium heavy saucepan.

2. Combine eggnog, corn syrup, butter and sugar in prepared saucepan. Cook over medium heat, stirring constantly, until sugar dissolves and mixture comes to a boil. Frequently wash down side of pan with pastry brush dipped in hot water to remove sugar crystals.

3. Attach candy thermometer to side of pan, making sure bulb is submerged in sugar mixture but not touching bottom of pan. Continue to cook until mixture reaches soft-ball stage (238°F).

4. Pour mixture into large heatproof bowl. Cool to lukewarm (about 110°F).

5. Add vanilla; beat with electric mixer until thick. Spread in prepared pan. Score fudge into 36 squares. Refrigerate until firm. Cut into squares.

Makes 36 pieces

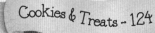

Molasses Spice Cookies

1¾ cups all-purpose flour

1 teaspoon baking soda

1 teaspoon ground ginger

1 teaspoon ground cinnamon

¼ teaspoon ground cloves

¼ teaspoon salt

1 cup granulated sugar

¾ cup (1½ sticks) butter or margarine, softened

1 egg

¼ cup unsulphured molasses

2 cups (12-ounce package) NESTLÉ® TOLL HOUSE® Premier White Morsels

1 cup finely chopped walnuts

COMBINE flour, baking soda, ginger, cinnamon, cloves and salt in small bowl. Beat sugar and butter in large mixer bowl until creamy. Beat in egg and molasses. Gradually beat in flour mixture. Stir in morsels. Refrigerate for 20 minutes or until slightly firm.

PREHEAT oven to 375°F.

ROLL dough into 1-inch balls; roll in walnuts. Place on ungreased baking sheets.

BAKE for 9 to 11 minutes or until golden brown. Cool on baking sheets for 2 minutes; remove to wire racks to cool completely.

Makes about 2½ dozen cookies

Dreamy Divinity

3½ cups DOMINO® Granulated Sugar

⅔ cup water

⅔ cup light corn syrup

⅓ teaspoon salt

3 egg whites, beaten until stiff

1½ teaspoons vanilla extract

Food coloring, candied cherries and chopped nuts (optional)

Combine sugar, water, corn syrup and salt in saucepan. Heat, stirring occasionally, until sugar dissolves. Wipe down sugar crystals from side of pan, as necessary, with pastry brush dipped in water. Without stirring, boil syrup mixture until it reaches 265°F or hard-ball stage on candy thermometer.

Gradually beat hot syrup into beaten egg whites. Add vanilla. Tint with food coloring, if desired. Continue beating until candy holds shape. Drop by teaspoonfuls onto buttered baking sheet or plate. Garnish with cherries and nuts as desired. When firm, store in airtight container. *Makes 50 pieces (1½ pounds)*

Chocolate Fudge-Peanut Butter Balls

2 cups (11½ ounces) milk chocolate chips

¼ cup half-and-half

⅓ cup creamy peanut butter

⅓ cup chopped peanuts

1. Melt chips with half-and-half in medium heavy saucepan over low heat, stirring occasionally. Whisk in peanut butter until blended. Refrigerate until mixture is firm enough to shape into balls but still soft, about 30 minutes, stirring occasionally.

2. Spread peanuts on waxed paper. Shape scant tablespoonfuls peanut butter mixture into 1-inch balls. Roll balls in peanuts. Store in refrigerator. *Makes about 32 balls*

Nonna's Holiday Biscotti

4 cups all-purpose flour, sifted

1 cup sugar

4 teaspoons baking powder

¼ teaspoon salt

4 eggs, lightly beaten

½ cup vegetable oil

2 teaspoons pure anise extract

1. Preheat oven to 350°F. Line cookie sheets with parchment paper.

2. Combine flour, sugar, baking powder and salt in large bowl. Make well in center of flour mixture. Pour eggs, oil and anise extract into well. Stir gradually, working flour mixture into dough. When too stiff to stir, turn out onto floured surface. Knead with floured hands until stiff dough forms; knead 5 minutes more. Shape into smooth loaf.

3. Working with ¼ of dough at a time, roll between palms to form rope about ½ inch in diameter. Cut into 6-inch lengths. Twist into pretzel shapes (bring ends of each piece together to form a loop; twist ends, then fold onto center of loop), or tie into knots. Place on prepared cookie sheets.

4. Bake 10 to 12 minutes on bottom rack of oven. Move to middle rack; bake 10 to 12 minutes. Cool 2 minutes on cookie sheets. Remove to wire racks; cool completely.   *Makes about 4 dozen cookies*

Pies, Cakes & More

Pumpkin Pecan Pie

1 can (15 ounces) solid-pack pumpkin

1 can (14 ounces) sweetened condensed milk

¼ cup (½ stick) butter, softened

2 eggs, divided

1 teaspoon ground cinnamon

1 teaspoon vanilla

½ teaspoon ground nutmeg

¼ teaspoon salt

1 (9-inch) graham cracker crust

2 tablespoons packed brown sugar

2 tablespoons dark corn syrup

1 tablespoon butter, melted

½ teaspoon maple flavoring

1 cup chopped pecans

1. Preheat oven to 400°F. Combine pumpkin, condensed milk, softened butter, 1 egg, cinnamon, vanilla, nutmeg and salt in large bowl. Pour into pie crust. Bake 20 minutes.

2. Beat remaining egg, brown sugar, corn syrup, melted butter and maple flavoring in medium bowl with electric mixer at medium speed until well blended. Stir in pecans.

3. Remove pie from oven; top with pecan mixture. *Reduce oven temperature to 350°F.* Bake 25 minutes or until knife inserted near center comes out clean. *Makes 8 to 10 servings*

Pumpkin Pecan Pie

Golden Apple Mincemeat Cake

3 cups flour

4 teaspoons baking powder

1 teaspoon ground allspice

1 teaspoon ground cinnamon

½ teaspoon salt

1½ cups vegetable oil

1½ cups packed brown sugar

2 cups grated Washington Golden Delicious apples

1 cup prepared mincemeat

½ cup chopped pecans

1½ teaspoons vanilla

3 eggs

1 to 2 tablespoons powdered sugar

Hard Sauce (recipe follows)

Preheat oven to 350°F. Combine flour, baking powder, allspice, cinnamon and salt in large bowl; set aside. In large bowl of electric mixer, combine oil and brown sugar; beat well. Add half the flour mixture; mix well. Blend in grated apples, mincemeat, pecans and vanilla. Add remaining flour mixture. Add eggs, 1 at a time; beat well after each addition. Turn into greased 10-inch Bundt pan. Bake 1 hour or until wooden toothpick inserted near center comes out clean. Cool in pan 15 minutes; turn out onto wire rack. When cool, sprinkle with powdered sugar. If desired, cake can be served slightly warm with Hard Sauce. *Makes 16 servings*

Hard Sauce: Beat ½ cup margarine and ⅛ teaspoon salt until light and fluffy. Gradually beat in 1 cup powdered sugar. Stir in 1 tablespoon brandy. Refrigerate 1 hour.

*Favorite recipe from **Washington Apple Commission***

Creamy Eggnog Dessert

Crust

1 package DUNCAN HINES® Moist Deluxe® Swiss Chocolate or
German Chocolate Cake Mix

½ cup (1 stick) butter or margarine, melted

½ cup chopped pecans

Filling

1 package (8 ounces) cream cheese, softened

1 cup granulated sugar

1 container (12 ounces) frozen whipped topping, thawed, divided

Topping

2 packages (4-serving size each) French vanilla-flavor instant
pudding and pie filling mix

3 cups cold milk

¼ teaspoon rum extract

¼ teaspoon ground nutmeg

1. Preheat oven to 350°F.

2. For crust, combine cake mix, melted butter and pecans in large
bowl. Reserve ½ cup mixture. Press remaining mixture onto bottom
of *ungreased* 13×9-inch pan. Bake 15 to 20 minutes or until surface is
firm. Cool. Toast reserved ½ cup mixture on cookie sheet 3 to
4 minutes, stirring once. Cool completely. Break lumps with fork to
make small crumbs.

3. For filling, combine cream cheese and sugar in large bowl; beat
until smooth. Stir in 1 cup whipped topping. Spread over cooled
crust. Refrigerate.

4. For topping, combine pudding mix and milk; beat 1 minute. Add
rum extract and nutmeg. Spread over cheese layer. Spread remaining
whipped topping over pudding layer. Sprinkle with reserved crumbs.
Refrigerate at least 2 hours.   *Makes 12 to 16 servings*

Holiday Cherry Coffeecake

3½ to 4 cups bread flour, divided*

1 cup plus 4 tablespoons sugar, divided

¼ cup powdered skim milk

1 package active dry yeast

1½ teaspoons salt

¾ cup water (120° to 130°F)

2 eggs

¼ cup (½ stick) butter or margarine, softened

1 (8-ounce) package cream cheese

1 (21-ounce) can cherry pie filling, divided

Two pounds frozen dough can be substituted for bread dough recipe. Thaw until soft and easy to roll.

In large bowl, combine 1½ cups flour, ⅓ cup sugar, powdered milk, yeast and salt. Add water, eggs and butter. Beat 3 minutes. Gradually stir in remaining flour until soft dough is formed. Turn dough onto floured surface; knead until smooth, about 10 minutes.

Place dough in bowl that has been coated with nonstick cooking spray, turning to grease top. Cover and let rise in warm place until doubled. Punch dough down; divide in half. Roll out half of dough into 24×6-inch rectangle. Combine cream cheese and ⅔ cup sugar; spread half of mixture down center of dough, leaving a 2½-inch margin on each side. Spoon half of cherry pie filling over top, leaving 1-inch margin at both ends. Fold one long side of dough over filling; fold opposite side of dough to overlap. Seal edges.

Place one end of pastry, seam side down, in center of 9-inch round baking pan well-coated with nonstick cooking spray. Wrap pastry loosely to form a coil; flatten dough slightly. Starting at center of coil, make deep slashes 1 inch apart along top of dough. Sprinkle 2 tablespoons sugar over dough. Repeat with remaining half of dough. Cover and let rise in a warm place 1 hour or until doubled in bulk. Bake at 350°F for 35 to 40 minutes or until golden brown. Let cool 15 to 20 minutes before removing from pan.   *Makes 2 coffeecakes (24 servings)*

*Favorite recipe from **North Dakota Wheat Commission***

Spicy Gingerbread
with Cinnamon-Pear Sauce

2 cups all-purpose flour

1 cup light molasses

¾ cup buttermilk

½ cup packed light brown sugar

½ cup (1 stick) butter, softened

1 teaspoon baking soda

1 teaspoon *each* ground ginger and ground cinnamon

¼ teaspoon salt

¼ teaspoon ground cloves

Cinnamon-Pear Sauce (recipe follows)

1. Preheat oven to 325°F. Grease and lightly flour 9-inch square baking pan; set aside.

2. Combine all ingredients except Cinnamon Pear Sauce in large bowl. Beat with electric mixer at low speed until well blended, frequently scraping down side of bowl with rubber spatula. Beat at high speed 2 minutes. Pour into prepared pan.

3. Bake 50 to 55 minutes or until toothpick inserted into center comes out clean. Cool in pan on wire rack about 30 minutes. Cut into squares; serve warm with Cinnamon-Pear Sauce.   *Makes 9 servings*

Cinnamon-Pear Sauce

2 cans (16 ounces each) pear halves in syrup, undrained

2 tablespoons granulated sugar

1 teaspoon fresh lemon juice

½ teaspoon ground cinnamon

Drain pear halves, reserving ¼ cup syrup. Place pears, reserved syrup, sugar, lemon juice and cinnamon in food processor or blender container; process until smooth. Just before serving, heat pear sauce in medium saucepan over medium heat until warm.   *Makes 2 cups sauce*

Holiday Fudge Torte

1 cup all-purpose flour

¾ cup sugar

¼ cup HERSHEY'S Cocoa

1½ teaspoons powdered instant coffee

¾ teaspoon baking soda

¼ teaspoon salt

½ cup (1 stick) butter or margarine, softened

¾ cup dairy sour cream

1 egg

½ teaspoon vanilla extract

Fudge Nut Glaze (recipe follows)

1. Heat oven to 350°F. Grease 9-inch round baking pan; line bottom with wax paper. Grease paper; flour paper and pan.

2. Stir together flour, sugar, cocoa, instant coffee, baking soda and salt in large bowl. Add butter, sour cream, egg and vanilla; beat on low speed of mixer until blended. Increase speed to medium; beat 3 minutes. Pour batter into prepared pan.

3. Bake 30 to 35 minutes or until wooden pick inserted into center comes out clean. Cool 10 minutes. Remove from pan to wire rack; gently peel off wax paper. Cool completely.

4. Prepare Fudge Nut Glaze.

5. Place cake on serving plate; pour glaze evenly over cake, allowing some to run down side. Refrigerate until glaze is firm, about 1 hour. Cover; refrigerate leftover torte.   *Makes 8 to 10 servings*

Fudge Nut Glaze

½ cup whipping cream

¼ cup sugar

1 tablespoon butter

1½ teaspoons light corn syrup

⅓ cup HERSHEY'S Semi-Sweet Chocolate Chips

¾ cup chopped MAUNA LOA® Macadamia Nuts, hazelnuts or pecans

½ teaspoon vanilla extract

1. Combine all ingredients except nuts and vanilla in small saucepan. Cook over medium heat, stirring constantly, until mixture boils. Cook, stirring constantly, 5 minutes. Remove from heat.

2. Cool 10 minutes; stir in nuts and vanilla.

Chocolate Glazed Pears

3 cups water

½ cup sugar

1 (2-inch) lemon peel twist

6 USA Bosc pears

6 ounces semi-sweet baking chocolate

2 tablespoons shortening

Combine water, sugar and lemon twist in large saucepan; bring to a boil. Pare pears and trim slightly to level bottom; remove core from blossom end, leaving stem intact. Add pears to poaching liquid; reduce heat. Cover and simmer gently about 8 to 10 minutes or until tender when pierced with tip of sharp knife; turn and baste occasionally. Remove pears from liquid; stand on flat dish. Cool. Melt chocolate and shortening in small saucepan over very low heat. Dry pears with paper towels. Holding each pear carefully by stem, spoon chocolate mixture over pear to coat. Let stand in cool place to set chocolate. Arrange pears on serving dish.   *Makes 6 servings*

Favorite recipe from Pear Bureau Northwest

Caramel Pumpkin Flan

¾ cup sugar, divided

4 eggs

1 cup canned solid-pack pumpkin

1 teaspoon ground cinnamon

¼ teaspoon salt

¼ teaspoon ground ginger

¼ teaspoon ground allspice

¼ teaspoon ground nutmeg

1 cup half-and-half

½ teaspoon vanilla

Boiling water

1. Preheat oven to 350°F.

2. Melt ½ cup sugar in 8-inch skillet over medium heat, stirring constantly, until sugar is caramelized. Immediately pour caramel syrup into 1-quart soufflé dish or other baking dish 7 to 8 inches in diameter. Tilt dish so caramel syrup flows over bottom and slightly up side. Let cool 10 minutes.

3. Beat eggs slightly in large bowl with electric mixer at medium speed. Add remaining ¼ cup sugar, pumpkin, cinnamon, salt, ginger, allspice and nutmeg. Beat until well blended. Add half-and-half and vanilla; beat until smooth. Pour over caramel syrup in dish. Set dish in larger pan. Pour boiling water into larger pan surrounding dish to depth of 1½ inches.

4. Bake 45 to 50 minutes or until knife inserted into center of flan comes out clean. Remove dish from water; place on wire rack to cool. Refrigerate, loosely covered, 6 hours or overnight.

5. To unmold flan, run knife around edge of dish. Cover with rimmed serving plate. Holding plate in place, invert dish. Flan and caramel syrup will slide onto plate. Cut into 6 wedges to serve; spoon caramel syrup over each wedge. *Makes 6 servings*

Apple Mince Pie

Prep Time: 30 minutes
Bake Time: 35 minutes

     Pastry for 2-crust pie
1 **(27-ounce) jar NONE SUCH® Ready-to-Use Mincemeat (Regular or Brandy & Rum)**
3 **medium all-purpose apples, cored, peeled and thinly sliced**
3 **tablespoons all-purpose flour**
2 **tablespoons butter or margarine, melted**
1 **egg yolk plus 2 tablespoons water, mixed**

1. Place rack in lower half of oven; preheat oven to 425°F.

2. In large bowl, toss apples with flour and butter; turn into prepared crust. Spoon NONE SUCH® evenly over apple mixture. Cover with top crust; cut slits near center. Seal and flute. Brush egg mixture over crust.

3. Bake 10 minutes. Reduce oven temperature to 375°F; bake 25 minutes longer or until golden. Cool. Garnish as desired. Store leftovers covered in refrigerator. *Makes one (9-inch) pie*

If you are unable to find mincemeat at your local store, this particular brand can also be purchased online.

Mini Pecan Tarts

Tart Shells

  2 cups all-purpose flour

  1 teaspoon granulated sugar

  Pinch salt

  ¾ cup (1½ sticks) cold butter or margarine, cut into pieces

  ⅓ cup ice water

Filling

  1 cup powdered sugar

  ½ cup (1 stick) butter

  ⅓ cup dark corn syrup

  1 cup chopped pecans

  36 pecan halves

1. For tart shells, combine flour, granulated sugar and salt in large bowl. Using pastry blender or two knives, cut ¾ cup cold butter into dry ingredients until mixture resembles crumbly corn meal. Add water, 1 tablespoon at a time, kneading mixture until dough forms a ball. Wrap dough in plastic wrap; flatten. Refrigerate at least 30 minutes.

2. Preheat oven to 375°F. Grease mini-muffin pans. Roll out dough on lightly floured surface to ⅛-inch thickness. Cut out 3-inch circles with cookie cutter; press into prepared mini-muffin cups. Bake about 8 minutes or until very lightly browned. Remove from oven. *Reduce oven temperature to 350°F.*

3. For filling, combine powdered sugar, ½ cup butter and corn syrup in 2-quart saucepan. Cook over medium heat, stirring occasionally, 4 to 5 minutes or until mixture comes to a full boil. Remove from heat; stir in chopped pecans. Spoon into warm baked shells. Top each with pecan half. Bake 5 minutes. Cool completely; remove from pans.

Makes 3 dozen tarts

Sweet and Spicy Fruitcake

    3 cups chopped walnuts
    2 cups chopped dried figs
    1 cup chopped dried apricots
    1 cup chocolate chips
 1½ cups flour, divided
    ¾ cup granulated sugar
    4 large eggs
    ¼ cup butter or margarine, softened
    ⅓ cup apple jelly
    2 tablespoons orange-flavor liqueur
    1 tablespoon grated orange peel
    1 tablespoon vanilla extract
    2 teaspoons TABASCO® brand Pepper Sauce
    1 teaspoon baking powder

Preheat oven to 325°F. Grease two 3-cup heat-safe bowls. Line bottoms and sides with foil; grease foil. Combine walnuts, figs, apricots, chocolate chips and ¼ cup flour in large bowl; mix well.

Beat sugar, eggs and butter in small bowl with mixer at low speed until well blended. Add jelly, remaining 1¼ cups flour and remaining ingredients. Beat at low speed until blended. Toss mixture with dried fruit in large bowl. Spoon into prepared bowls. Cover bowls with greased foil. Bake 40 minutes; uncover and bake 40 minutes or until toothpicks inserted into centers come out clean. Remove to wire racks to cool.

If desired, brush cooled fruitcakes with 1 tablespoon melted apple jelly and sprinkle each with 2 tablespoons finely chopped dried apricots. Store in cool place for up to 3 weeks.

Makes 2 small fruitcakes

Triple Chocolate Peppermint Cheesecake

Chocolate Crumb Crust (recipe follows)

1 cup (6 ounces) mint semisweet chocolate chips

1 cup (6 ounces) semisweet chocolate chips

¾ cup whipping cream

3 packages (8 ounces each) cream cheese, softened

¾ cup packed brown sugar

3 eggs

¼ cup unsweetened cocoa powder

1 teaspoon vanilla

Sweetened whipped cream

Crushed peppermint candy

1. Preheat oven to 325°F. Prepare Chocolate Crumb Crust; set aside.

2. Melt chocolates with cream in small heavy saucepan over low heat, stirring until smooth; set aside. Beat cream cheese in large bowl with electric mixer on medium speed until fluffy. Beat in brown sugar until light and fluffy. Beat in eggs, 1 at a time, on low speed until well blended. Stir in cocoa and vanilla. Blend chocolate mixture into cream cheese mixture on low speed, scraping side of bowl frequently. Spoon into prepared crust.

3. Bake 45 to 50 minutes or until center of cake is just set. Remove pan to wire rack. Carefully loosen edges of cake with thin knife. Cool completely on wire rack. Refrigerate several hours or overnight.

4. To serve, place on plate. Carefully remove side of pan. Place star tip in pastry bag; add sweetened whipped cream. Pipe rosettes on outside edge of cake. Sprinkle rosettes with crushed peppermint candy.

Makes 1 (9-inch) cheesecake

Chocolate Crumb Crust: Preheat oven to 325°F. Combine 1 cup chocolate wafer crumbs and 3 tablespoons melted butter or margarine in small bowl until well blended. Press onto bottom of 9-inch springform pan. Bake 10 minutes. Cool on wire rack while preparing filling.

Date Gingerbread

1¼ cups plus 1 teaspoon all-purpose flour, divided

¾ cup finely chopped pitted dates (about 18 whole dates)

½ cup whole wheat flour

¼ cup packed brown sugar

1 tablespoon (½ ounce) finely chopped candied ginger

½ teaspoon baking powder

½ teaspoon baking soda

½ teaspoon ground ginger

½ teaspoon ground nutmeg

½ cup water

½ cup molasses

¼ cup canola or vegetable oil

2 egg whites

Orange slices

1. Preheat oven to 350°F. Coat 8-inch round baking pan with nonstick cooking spray; dust with 1 teaspoon all-purpose flour. Set aside.

2. Combine remaining 1¼ cups all-purpose flour, dates, whole wheat flour, brown sugar, candied ginger, baking powder, baking soda, ground ginger and nutmeg in large bowl. Add water, molasses, oil and egg whites. Beat with electric mixer at low speed until combined. Increase speed to high; beat 2 minutes. Pour into prepared pan.

3. Bake 38 to 40 minutes or until toothpick inserted into center comes out clean. Cool in pan on wire rack 10 minutes. Cut into wedges; serve warm. Garnish with orange slices.   *Makes 8 servings*

Chocolate Cake Squares with Eggnog Sauce

1½ teaspoons baking soda

 1 cup buttermilk

¾ cup HERSHEY'S Cocoa

¾ cup boiling water

¼ cup (½ stick) butter or margarine, softened

¼ cup shortening

 2 cups sugar

 2 eggs

 1 teaspoon vanilla extract

⅛ teaspoon salt

1¾ cups all-purpose flour

　　Eggnog Sauce (recipe follows)

1. Heat oven to 350°F. Grease and flour 13×9×2-inch baking pan. Stir baking soda into buttermilk in medium bowl; set aside. Stir together cocoa and water until smooth; set aside.

2. Beat butter, shortening and sugar in large bowl until creamy. Add eggs, vanilla and salt; beat well. Add buttermilk mixture alternately with flour to butter mixture, beating until blended. Add cocoa mixture; blend thoroughly. Pour batter into prepared pan. Bake 40 to 45 minutes or until wooden pick inserted into center comes out clean. Cool completely. Serve with Eggnog Sauce.　　　　　　　　*Makes 12 to 15 servings*

Eggnog Sauce

 1 tablespoon cornstarch

1⅓ cups milk

¼ cup sugar

 3 egg yolks, beaten

¼ teaspoon *each* brandy and vanilla extracts

　　Several dashes ground nutmeg

1. Stir cornstarch with *2 tablespoons* cold water in medium until smooth. Add milk, sugar and egg yolks. Beat with whisk until well blended. Cook over medium heat, stirring constantly, until thickened. Remove from heat. Stir in extracts. Cool completely. Sprinkle nutmeg over top. Cover; refrigerate leftover sauce.

Makes about 1¾ cups sauce

Pumpkin Crunch Cake

1 package (18.25 ounces) yellow cake mix, *divided*

1⅔ cups LIBBY'S® Easy Pumpkin Pie Mix

2 large eggs

2 teaspoons pumpkin pie spice

⅓ cup flaked coconut

¼ cup chopped nuts

3 tablespoons butter or margarine, softened

PREHEAT oven to 350°F. Grease 13×9-inch baking pan.

COMBINE *3 cups* yellow cake mix, pumpkin pie mix, eggs and pumpkin pie spice in large mixer bowl. Beat on medium speed of electric mixer for 2 minutes. Pour into prepared baking pan.

COMBINE *remaining* cake mix, coconut and nuts in small bowl; cut in butter with pastry blender or two knives until mixture is crumbly. Sprinkle over batter.

BAKE for 30 to 35 minutes or until wooden pick inserted into center comes out clean. Cool in pan on wire rack. *Makes 20 servings*

Holiday Fruit Cake

1 pound diced candied mixed fruits

8 ounces candied cherries, cut into halves

4 ounces candied pineapple, chopped

1½ cups chopped nuts

1 cup raisins

½ cup all-purpose flour

1 package DUNCAN HINES® Moist Deluxe® Spice Cake Mix

1 package (4-serving size) vanilla-flavor instant pudding and pie filling mix

3 eggs

½ cup vegetable oil

¼ cup water

Light corn syrup, heated, for garnish

1. Preheat oven to 300°F. Grease 10-inch tube pan. Line bottom with aluminum foil.

2. Reserve ¼ cup assorted candied fruits and nuts for garnish, if desired. Combine remaining candied fruits, nuts and raisins in large bowl. Toss with flour until evenly coated. Set aside.

3. Combine cake mix, pudding mix, eggs, oil and water in large mixing bowl. Beat at medium speed with electric mixer for 3 minutes (batter will be very stiff). Stir in candied fruit mixture. Spread in prepared pan. Bake 2 hours or until toothpick inserted near center comes out clean. Cool completely in pan. Invert onto serving plate. Peel off foil.

4. Brush cake with hot corn syrup and decorate with reserved candied fruit pieces and nuts, if desired. To store, wrap in aluminum foil or plastic wrap, or place in airtight container.

Makes 20 to 24 servings

Cran-Raspberry Hazelnut Trifle

2 cups hazelnut-flavored liquid dairy creamer

1 package (4-serving size) vanilla instant pudding and pie filling mix

1 package (about 11 ounces) frozen pound cake, thawed

1 can (21 ounces) raspberry pie filling

1 can (16 ounces) whole berry cranberry sauce

1. Combine creamer and pudding mix in medium bowl; beat with wire whisk 1 to 2 minutes or until thickened.

2. Cut pound cake into ¾-inch cubes.

3. Combine pie filling and cranberry sauce in medium bowl; blend well.

4. Layer ⅓ of cake cubes, ¼ of fruit sauce and ⅓ of pudding mixture in 1½- to 2-quart straight-sided glass serving bowl. Repeat layers twice; top with remaining fruit sauce. Cover; refrigerate until serving time.

Makes 8 servings

Serve It With Style: Garnish trifle with whipped topping and fresh mint sprigs.

Trifles are meant to be served in glass bowls to show off their colorful layers.

Dried Fruit Compote

1 cup water

1 cup apple juice

½ cup Rhine wine or additional apple juice

¼ cup packed light brown sugar

2 cinnamon sticks

4 whole allspice berries

4 whole cloves

4 whole black peppercorns

1 package (8 ounces) dried mixed fruit

Fresh mint sprigs (optional)

1. Combine water, apple juice, wine and brown sugar in medium saucepan.

2. Wrap cinnamon sticks, allspice berries, cloves and peppercorns in 8-inch square of double-thickness cheesecloth. Tie securely with string. Add to saucepan. Stir in fruit.

3. Bring to a boil over high heat. Reduce heat to low; cover and simmer 12 to 15 minutes or until fruit is tender, stirring once. Cool; discard cheesecloth bag and spices.

4. Serve compote warm, at room temperature or chilled in small bowls. Garnish with fresh mint. *Makes 6 servings*

Note: This recipe can be prepared with ground spices instead of whole spices. Substitute ½ teaspoon ground cinnamon for cinnamon sticks, ¼ teaspoon ground allspice for allspice berries, ⅛ teaspoon ground cloves for whole cloves and ⅛ teaspoon black pepper for peppercorns. Simply add the ground spices directly to the saucepan before stirring in the dried fruit.

Cranberry Apple Crisp

Prep Time: 25 minutes
Cook Time: 50 minutes

- ½ cup KARO® Light Corn Syrup
- ⅓ to ½ cup sugar
- 1 teaspoon cinnamon
- ½ teaspoon nutmeg
- 5 to 6 cups cubed peeled tart apples
- 1 cup fresh or frozen cranberries
- 3 tablespoons ARGO® or KINGSFORD'S® Corn Starch
- 1 teaspoon grated orange peel

Topping

- ½ cup walnuts or uncooked oats
- ⅓ cup packed brown sugar
- ¼ cup flour
- ¼ cup (½ stick) margarine or butter

1. Preheat oven to 350°F.

2. In large bowl combine Karo, sugar, cinnamon and nutmeg. Add apples, cranberries, corn starch and orange peel; toss to mix well. Spoon into shallow 2-quart baking dish.

3. For Topping: Combine nuts, brown sugar and flour. With pastry blender or 2 knives, cut in margarine until crumbly. Sprinkle over cranberry mixture.

4. Bake 50 minutes or until apples are tender and juices that bubble up in center are shiny and clear. Cool slightly; serve warm.

Makes 8 servings

Apple Brandy Praline Pie

Prep Time: 30 minutes
Bake Time: 50 minutes, plus cooling

    Praline Topping (recipe follows)
¼ **cup sugar**
3 **tablespoons all-purpose flour**
¼ **teaspoon salt**
3 **eggs**
½ **cup KARO® Light or Dark Corn Syrup**
¼ **cup (½ stick) margarine or butter, melted**
2 **tablespoons apple or plain brandy**
2 **medium apples, peeled and thinly sliced**
1 **unbaked (9-inch) pie crust**

1. Preheat oven to 350°F. Prepare Praline Topping; set aside.

2. In large bowl combine sugar, flour and salt. Beat in eggs, corn syrup, margarine and brandy. Stir in apples. Pour into pie crust.

3. Sprinkle with topping.

4. Bake 45 to 50 minutes or until puffed and set. Cool on wire rack.

Makes 8 servings

Praline Topping: In small bowl combine 1 cup coarsely chopped pecans, ¼ cup all-purpose flour, ¼ cup brown sugar and 2 tablespoons softened margarine or butter. Mix with fork until crumbly.

Streusel Topped Pumpkin Pie

1 (15-ounce) can pumpkin (2 cups)

1 (14-ounce) can EAGLE BRAND® Sweetened Condensed Milk
   (NOT evaporated milk)

1 egg

1¼ teaspoons ground cinnamon, divided

½ teaspoon salt

½ teaspoon ground ginger

½ teaspoon ground nutmeg

1 (8- or 9-inch) prepared graham cracker crust

¼ cup firmly packed light brown sugar

2 tablespoons all-purpose flour

2 tablespoons cold butter or margarine

¾ cup chopped walnuts

1. Preheat oven to 425°F. Whisk pumpkin, EAGLE BRAND®, egg, ¾ teaspoon cinnamon, salt, ginger and nutmeg in medium bowl. Pour into crust. Bake 15 minutes.

2. In small bowl, combine brown sugar, flour and remaining ½ teaspoon cinnamon; cut in butter until crumbly. Stir in walnuts. Remove pie from oven; reduce oven temperature to 350°F. Sprinkle streusel mixture over pie.

3. Bake 40 minutes or until set. Cool. Serve warm or at room temperature. Store leftovers covered in refrigerator.

Makes 1 (8- or 9-inch) pie

Serving Suggestion: Top with whipped cream, if desired.

New-Fashioned Gingerbread Cake

- 2 cups cake flour
- 1 teaspoon baking powder
- 1 teaspoon ground ginger
- ½ teaspoon baking soda
- ½ teaspoon ground cinnamon
- ½ teaspoon ground nutmeg
- ¼ teaspoon ground cloves
- ¾ cup water
- ⅓ cup packed brown sugar
- ¼ cup molasses
- 3 tablespoons canola oil
- 2 tablespoons finely minced crystallized ginger (optional)
- 2 tablespoons powdered sugar

1. Preheat oven to 350°F. Coat 8-inch square baking pan with nonstick cooking spray; set aside.

2. Combine flour, baking powder, ginger, baking soda, cinnamon, nutmeg and cloves in large bowl; mix well.

3. Beat water, brown sugar, molasses and oil in small bowl with electric mixer at low speed until well blended. Pour into flour mixture; beat until just blended. Stir in crystallized ginger. Pour into prepared pan.

4. Bake 30 to 35 minutes or until toothpick inserted into center comes out clean. Let cool 10 minutes. Sprinkle with powdered sugar just before serving. *Makes 9 servings*

Peppermint Cheesecake

Crust

1¼ cups vanilla wafer crumbs

3 tablespoons melted margarine

Filling

4 cups (30 ounces) SARGENTO® Light Ricotta Cheese

½ cup sugar

½ cup half-and-half

¼ cup all-purpose flour

1 teaspoon vanilla

¼ teaspoon salt

3 eggs

16 peppermint candies

Fresh mint leaves (optional)

Lightly grease sides of 8- or 9-inch springform pan. Combine crumbs and margarine; mix well. Press evenly onto bottom of pan. Refrigerate while preparing filling. Combine Ricotta cheese, sugar, half-and-half, flour, vanilla and salt in large bowl; beat with electric mixer until smooth. Add eggs, one at a time; beat until smooth. Place candies in heavy plastic bag. Crush with meat mallet or hammer. Reserve ¼ cup larger pieces for garnish; stir remaining crushed candies into batter. Pour batter over crust. Bake at 350°F 1 hour or until center is just set. Turn off oven; cool in oven with door propped open 30 minutes. Remove to wire cooling rack; loosen cake from rim of pan with metal spatula. Cool completely; refrigerate at least 4 hours. Immediately before serving, garnish cake around top edge with reserved crushed candies and mint leaves, if desired. *Makes 8 servings*

Cranberry Bread Pudding

1 quart (4 cups) milk

2 cups sugar

1 cup dried sweetened cranberries

5 eggs, lightly beaten

2 tablespoons vanilla

1 tablespoon baking powder

½ teaspoon ground cinnamon

1 loaf (16 ounces) French bread, torn into small pieces

Brandy Sauce

1½ cups sugar

1 cup (2 sticks) butter or margarine

½ cup milk

½ to ¾ cup brandy

1. Preheat oven to 350°F. Spray 13×9-inch baking dish with nonstick cooking spray.

2. Combine 1 quart milk, 2 cups sugar, cranberries, eggs, vanilla, baking powder and cinnamon in large bowl; stir until well blended. Add bread; toss to combine. Pour mixture into prepared dish. Bake 50 to 70 minutes or until golden and toothpick inserted into center comes out clean.

3. Meanwhile, prepare Brandy Sauce. Combine 1½ cups sugar, butter and ½ cup milk in small saucepan. Heat over medium-high heat, stirring frequently, until sugar dissolves. Remove from heat. Stir in brandy.

4. Cut bread pudding into squares. Serve with sauce.

Makes 12 servings

Plum Pudding Pie

⅓ cup plus 2 tablespoons KAHLÚA® Liqueur

½ cup golden raisins

½ cup chopped pitted dates

⅓ cup chopped candied cherries

½ cup chopped walnuts

⅓ cup dark corn syrup

½ teaspoon pumpkin pie spice

¼ cup butter or margarine, softened

¼ cup packed brown sugar

2 tablespoons all-purpose flour

¼ teaspoon salt

2 eggs, lightly beaten

1 (9-inch) unbaked pie shell

1 cup whipping cream

Maraschino cherries (optional)

In medium bowl, combine ⅓ cup Kahlúa®, raisins, dates and cherries; mix well. Cover; let stand 1 to 4 hours. Stir in walnuts, corn syrup and spice. In large bowl, cream butter, sugar, flour and salt. Stir in eggs. Add fruit mixture; blend well. Pour into unbaked pie shell. Bake in preheated 350°F oven 35 minutes or until filling is firm and crust is golden. Cool completely on wire rack. When ready to serve, in small bowl, beat whipping cream with remaining 2 tablespoons Kahlua® just until soft peaks form. Spoon cream into pastry bag fitted with large star tip and pipe decoratively over top of dessert. If desired, garnish with maraschino cherries.   *Makes 8 servings*

The publisher would like to thank the companies and organizations listed below for the use of their recipes and photographs in this publication.

ACH Food Companies, Inc.

American Lamb Council

Birds Eye Foods

Cabot® Creamery Cooperative

Chef Paul Prudhomme's Magic Seasoning Blends®

Cherry Marketing Institute

Crisco is a registered trademark of The J.M. Smucker Company

Del Monte Corporation

Dole Food Company, Inc.

Domino® Foods, Inc.

Duncan Hines® and Moist Deluxe® are registered trademarks of Pinnacle Foods Corp.

EAGLE BRAND®

Grandma's® is a registered trademark of Mott's, LLP

The Hershey Company

The Hidden Valley® Food Products Company

Jennie-O Turkey Store®

Kahlúa® Liqueur

MASTERFOODS USA

McIlhenny Company (TABASCO® brand Pepper Sauce)

Mott's® is a registered trademark of Mott's, LLP

National Honey Board

National Pork Board

National Turkey Federation

Nestlé USA

New York Apple Association, Inc.

Norseland, Inc.

Lucini Italia Co.

North Dakota Wheat Commission

Pear Bureau Northwest

Perdue Farms Incorporated

Reckitt Benckiser Inc.

Riviana Foods Inc.

Sargento® Foods Inc.

The Sugar Association, Inc.

Unilever Foods North America

USA Dry Pea & Lentil Council

USA Rice Federation

Washington Apple Commission

METRIC CONVERSION CHART

VOLUME MEASUREMENTS (dry)

1/8 teaspoon = 0.5 mL
1/4 teaspoon = 1 mL
1/2 teaspoon = 2 mL
3/4 teaspoon = 4 mL
1 teaspoon = 5 mL
1 tablespoon = 15 mL
2 tablespoons = 30 mL
1/4 cup = 60 mL
1/3 cup = 75 mL
1/2 cup = 125 mL
2/3 cup = 150 mL
3/4 cup = 175 mL
1 cup = 250 mL
2 cups = 1 pint = 500 mL
3 cups = 750 mL
4 cups = 1 quart = 1 L

VOLUME MEASUREMENTS (fluid)

1 fluid ounce (2 tablespoons) = 30 mL
4 fluid ounces (1/2 cup) = 125 mL
8 fluid ounces (1 cup) = 250 mL
12 fluid ounces (1 1/2 cups) = 375 mL
16 fluid ounces (2 cups) = 500 mL

WEIGHTS (mass)

1/2 ounce = 15 g
1 ounce = 30 g
3 ounces = 90 g
4 ounces = 120 g
8 ounces = 225 g
10 ounces = 285 g
12 ounces = 360 g
16 ounces = 1 pound = 450 g

DIMENSIONS

1/16 inch = 2 mm
1/8 inch = 3 mm
1/4 inch = 6 mm
1/2 inch = 1.5 cm
3/4 inch = 2 cm
1 inch = 2.5 cm

OVEN TEMPERATURES

250°F = 120°C
275°F = 140°C
300°F = 150°C
325°F = 160°C
350°F = 180°C
375°F = 190°C
400°F = 200°C
425°F = 220°C
450°F = 230°C

BAKING PAN SIZES

Utensil	Size in Inches/Quarts	Metric Volume	Size in Centimeters
Baking or Cake Pan (square or rectangular)	8×8×2	2 L	20×20×5
	9×9×2	2.5 L	23×23×5
	12×8×2	3 L	30×20×5
	13×9×2	3.5 L	33×23×5
Loaf Pan	8×4×3	1.5 L	20×10×7
	9×5×3	2 L	23×13×7
Round Layer Cake Pan	8×1½	1.2 L	20×4
	9×1½	1.5 L	23×4
Pie Plate	8×1¼	750 mL	20×3
	9×1¼	1 L	23×3
Baking Dish or Casserole	1 quart	1 L	—
	1½ quart	1.5 L	—
	2 quart	2 L	—